D0461388

*"Of all the dogs that are so sweet,*
*The spaniel is the most complete . . . ."*
—E.V. Lucas, *The More I See of Men . . .*, 1927

# Love of
# Spaniels

The Ultimate Tribute to Cockers, Springers,
and Other Great Spaniels

Todd R. Berger, Editor

With stories by James Herriot,
Virginia Woolf, Barbara Bush,
E.V. Lucas, Horace Lytle, and others

Voyageur Press

PetLife
LIBRARY

## *Dedication*

To Ron Guelzow

Compiled and edited by Todd R. Berger
Designed by Kjerstin Moody
Printed in Hong Kong

00  01  02  03  04  5  4  3  2  1

**Library of Congress Cataloging-in-Publication Data**

Love of spaniels : the ultimate tribute to cockers, springers, and other great spaniels / Todd R. Berger, editor ; with stories by James Herriot . . . [et al.].
    p. cm. — (PetLife library)
    ISBN 0-89658-453-4
    1. Spaniels—Anecdotes. 2. Spaniels—Pictorial works.
    3. Dog owners—Anecdotes. I. Berger, Todd R., 1968–
    II. Herriot, James. III. Series.

    SF429.S7L68 2000
    636.752'4—dc21

Distributed in Canada by Raincoast Books, 9050 Shaughnessy Street, Vancouver, B.C. V6P 6E5

Published by Voyageur Press, Inc.
123 North Second Street, P.O. Box 338
Stillwater, MN 55082 U.S.A.
651-430-2210, fax 651-430-2211
books@voyageurpress.com
www.voyageurpress.com

*Educators, fundraisers, premium and gift buyers, publicists, and marketing managers:* Looking for creative products and new sales ideas? Voyageur Press books are available at special discounts when purchased in quantities, and special editions can be created to your specifications. For details contact the marketing department at 800-888-9653.

**Permissions**

We have made every effort to determine original sources and locate copyright holders of the excerpts in this book. Grateful acknowledgment is made to the writers, publishers, and agencies listed below for permission to reprint material copyrighted or controlled by them. Please bring to our attention any errors of fact, omission, or copyright.

"The Dimmocks" from *James Herriot's Dog Stories* by James Herriot. Copyright © 1986 by James Herriot. Reprinted in the United States by permission of St. Martin's Press, LLC. Reprinted in all other territories by permission of David Higham Associates.

"The Back Bedroom" from *Flush: A Biography* by Virginia Woolf. Copyright © 1933 by Harcourt, Inc. and renewed 1961 by Leonard Woolf. Reprinted in the United States by permission of Harcourt, Inc. Reprinted in all other territories by permission of The Society of Authors as the literary representative for the Estate of Virginia Woolf.

"A China Dog" from *C. Fred's Story* by C. Fred Bush (Edited slightly by Barbara Bush). Copyright © 1984 by Barbara Bush. Reprinted by permission of Doubleday, a division of Random House, Inc.

"The Heart of My Hunting" by Charles A. Fergus. Originally appeared in *A Breed Apart: A Tribute to the Hunting Dogs that Own our Souls*, edited by Doug Truax. Copyright © 1993 and 1994 by Countrysport, Inc. Reprinted by permission of Countrysport, Inc.

"The Lord of Life" from *"The More I See of Men . . ."* by E.V. Lucas. Copyright © 1927 by E.V. Lucas. Reprinted by permission of Methuen Publishing Ltd.

"Ruffled Paws" from *A Sense of Humus* by Bertha Damon. Copyright © 1943 by Bertha Damon. Copyright © renewed 1970 by Bertha Damon. Reprinted by permission of Simon & Schuster.

Page 1: *A happy-as-a-clam American cocker spaniel puppy soaks up the sunshine on a warm summer afternoon.* Photograph © Sharon Eide/Elizabeth Flynn

Page 2-3: *Autumn in Montana: time for a springer to go afield.* Photograph © Alan and Sandy Carey

Page 3 inset: *A Blenheim (chestnut and white) Cavalier King Charles spaniel poses with its friend: a fire hydrant.* Photograph © Kent and Donna Dannen

Facing page: *An English cocker spaniel retrieves the daily news.* Photograph © Tara Darling

Page 6: *A champion Welsh springer spaniel.* Photograph © Judith E. Strom

# Contents

# Introduction

 "What is a spaniel?" seems like a pretty straightforward question, but, in fact, is not a straightforward query at all. Sure, "spaniel" signifies a family of dogs, dogs with an ingrown trait of supreme merriness and an inherent love for their owners. Everyone from a four-year-old child to my eighty-three-year-old grandpa knows well what a spaniel is: It's that happy cocker gobbling up a sandwich especially prepared for him; it's an English springer flushing a pheasant for the gun; it's a lumbering Clumber spaniel moving slowly like a Basset hound across the lawn.

But it is in precisely these things that the problem of defining a "spaniel" crops up: Spaniels are all of these things, as spaniels come in all shapes and sizes, with all kinds of talents and traits. In fact, there is more variation in size and appearance in spaniels than any other dog family. These big and small dogs even have similar names, such as the American water spaniel and Irish water spaniel, English springer spaniel and Welsh springer spaniel, English cocker spaniel and American cocker spaniel. Some spaniels that once stood by their masters are no longer around today, including the alpine spaniel and the English water spaniel. And just to muddy the waters further, several breeds commonly called "spaniels" are not really spaniels at all.

It seems a little history of the spaniels is needed to try to clear things up.

*Bedraggled and bandannaed, an American cocker spaniel patiently surveys the surroundings while its owner is preoccupied.* Photograph © Kent and Donna Dannen

## A Brief History of Spaniels

Spaniels date back two thousand years, at least in some spaniel-like form. They were probably around when the Roman Empire was at its peak, evidenced by carvings in Roman ruins of a dog similar to today's water spaniel. In fact, spaniels likely have the longest lineage of any family of dogs that has survived to modern times. Not surprisingly, the history of spaniels is complicated, especially given this long lineage. But their history is also colorful, with odd tales of spaniels showing up at key moments in the history of the world.

There seems little doubt that the true spaniels originated in Spain. History books from the 1300s indicate the existence of "Spaynells" on the Iberian Peninsula, and the breed makes an appearance in other writings as well, including Gaston de Foix's *Livre de Chasse* (1387) and Dame Julyan Barnes's *The Book of St. Albans* (1486), as well as in the work of Geoffrey Chaucer and, later, William Shakespeare. Spaniels—often toy spaniels—also turned up in the work of many of the great painters, including Titian, Anthony Van Dyck, Rembrandt van Rijn, and Sir Edwin Landseer.

It was around the fourteenth century that spaniels were first used for hunting, a task that became the foundation for development of the family. Many years later, William Taplin explained quite well in his book *The Sporting Dictionary and Rural Repository* (1803) why this breed was often chosen to go afield: "[Spaniels] are indefatigable in their exertions. From the time they are thrown off in the pursuit of game, the tail is a perpetual motion . . . by the increased volume of which an experienced sportsman knows when he gets nearer the object of attraction. The nearer he approaches it, the more violent he becomes in his endeavors to succeed; tremulative whimpers escape him as a matter of doubt; but the moment that doubt's dispelled, his clamorous raptures break forth in full confirmation of the gratification he receives."

Categorization of these dogs into something further than the all-encompassing term "spaniels" began with the publication of Dr. Johannes Caius's *A Treatise on Englishe Dogges* in 1576. Caius, a Cambridge University professor, grouped the "Spaniells" into land and water spaniels, the former lumped together with setters and various French dogs and the latter believed to be some kind of archaic poodle, which was also called a "Fynder." Though the land spaniels gradually became known as the "field" spaniels, these distinctions would be the basis of the division of the spaniel tribes for several hundred years.

Another spaniel noted by Caius, the "Spaniell Gentle," was the likely ancestor of today's Cavalier King Charles spaniel, the lapdog that originated as a land spaniel but developed in the sixteenth and seventeenth century as a "Comforte Dog." The British aristocracy would often ride around in their carriages on cold London nights with a toy spaniel snuggled in their laps for warmth. These lapdogs also had another practical role: They attracted fleas and other vermin away from their owners, not a bad idea in the days of the Black Death. The name

Facing page: *The merry nature of the English springer spaniel—or pretty much any spaniel for that matter—radiates from this happy hound galloping across a field.*
Photograph © Daniel Dempster

of the breed, by the way, stems from Charles II, the King of England from 1660 to 1685, who was never without his toy spaniel.

According to Gerald and Loretta Hausman in their book *The Mythology of Dogs*, a spaniel may actually have been responsible for the founding of the Anglican Church. It seems Henry VIII, the King of England from 1509 to 1547, sent his ambassador Lord Wiltshire to see Pope Clement VII to gain papal approval of the annulment of Henry's marriage to Catherine of Aragon. Upon meeting the pontiff, the lord knelt to kiss the papal foot. A sudden movement by the pope startled Lord Wiltshire's spaniel, who had accompanied his master, and the hound promptly bit the leader of the Catholics on the toe. The pope sent the lord on his way, and upon Lord Wiltshire's return to England without the papal approval of his annulment, Henry VIII founded the Church of England, with himself as "Protector and Supreme Head." He then simply approved the annulment himself.

Throughout the 1600s, spaniels of one type or another just seemed to keep turning up. A spaniel was aboard the Mayflower when it struck land in 1620, and in the latter half of the century, Jean de la Fontaine wrote of a spaniel in his fable "The Little Dog."

It was not until the rise of dog shows in Europe in the 1800s, however, that the distinctions made three hundred years earlier by Johannes Caius were further defined, placing the spaniels into categories familiar to the modern spaniel lover. At first the field spaniels

*A Scottish sportsman and a pack of English cockers head afield. English cocker spaniels, a wholly separate breed from the American cocker spaniel that is more common in the United States, is one of the most popular breeds in the United Kingdom.* Photograph © Gary Kramer

(called land spaniels by Caius) were divided by size, with dogs under twenty-five pounds named "cocking spaniels," while those heavier than twenty-five pounds that were multicolored were called "springing spaniels" and the solid-colored ones retained the name "field spaniels." The name "cocking spaniel" derived from the breed's specialty as a woodcock hunter, while the "springing spaniel" (sometimes inaccurately called the Norfolk spaniel) derived from the springer's hunting style, as the dog would spring forward to flush game for the hunter.

By the end of the 1800s, the Kennel Club of Great Britain formalized the split between the cocker spaniel and the field spaniel, slotting the breeds into separate categories in 1894. The English springer spaniel received a similar nod in 1902. Thereafter, the other spaniels (including the Welsh springer spaniel, Irish water spaniel, Cavalier King Charles spaniel, Clumber spaniel, and Sussex spaniel) also won their own classifications.

Cockers developed further during the twentieth century, as the dogs on either side of the Atlantic diverged. The distinction between the American cocker spaniel and the English cocker spaniel led to a decision in 1938 to stop interbreeding of the two cockers, and a formal decision by the American Kennel Club in 1946 recognized the English cocker as a separate breed. Incidentally, the American cocker is known simply as the cocker in the United States, while elsewhere the English cocker is the cocker and the American cocker is the breed further distinguished.

Three breeds that do not make the list of official spaniels are the cause of some confusion. Until relatively recently, the Brittany was known as the Brittany spaniel and is still called such in many circles. But the talented and popular gun dog is much more setterlike, pointing game in the field instead of flushing like the spaniels.

*The rare American water spaniel, developed in the American midwest, is a talented waterfowler.* Photograph © Judith E. Strom

Though the Brittany likely has spaniel (as well as setter and pointer) ancestors, officially the gorgeous dog is not a spaniel.

The Tibetan spaniel does retain the name spaniel, though the dog is not a spaniel at all. The precise origins of this breed are not quite clear, though they are native to Tibet where they were companion dogs to monks and lamas. They are likely related to other Tibetan breeds such as the Lhasa Apso rather than any of the true spaniels.

And lastly, the German spaniel, also known as the Deutscher Wachtelhund and the German quail dog, may or may not have spaniel blood, as its origin is quite murky. The breed does have the look of a brown English springer spaniel, but is little known outside of Germany. In fact, the American Kennel Club and the Kennel Club of Great Britain do not recognize the breed.

So, to sum up, the spaniels that you will see in these pages—some with stories and all with photographs—are the American and English cocker spaniels, American and Irish water spaniels, the English and Welsh springer spaniels, the field spaniel, the Clumber spaniel, the Sussex spaniel, and the Cavalier King Charles spaniel. Feel free to love your Brittany, Deutscher Wachtelhund, or Tibetan spaniel all you like—and these breeds, like dogs everywhere, are acutely worthy of your love. But these wonderful dogs do not make an appearance in *Love of Spaniels.*

## About *Love of Spaniels*

*Love of Spaniels* is a first-of-its-kind tribute to spaniels, a group of dogs worthy, individually or collectively, of a thousand such testimonials. Through words and images, *Love of Spaniels* gives a little back to the happy hounds that share our lives.

Great writers have lifted their pens to write of spaniels, and, indeed, here you will read the work of Richard Burton, James Herriot, Virginia Woolf, Barbara Bush, Paul A. Curtis, Charles Fergus, E.V. Lucas, Bertha Damon, and Horace Lytle. Amidst the words of these writers, the spirit of the spaniel resides.

The spirit is also evident in the image, and the work of the great spaniel photographers fill these pages. *Love of Spaniels* includes photographs by Bryan and Cherry Alexander, Norvia Behling, Alan and Sandy Carey, Kent and Donna Dannen, Tara Darling, Daniel Dempster, Sharon Eide and Elizabeth Flynn, Isabelle Francais, Barbara von Hoffmann, Bill Kinney, Gary Kramer, William H. Mullins, Robert and Eunice Pearcy, Ron Spomer, Judith E. Strom, and Marilyn "Angel" Wynn.

You know you love the spaniel by your side. But this isn't a how-to book: You've already got the loving your spaniel part down. *Love of Spaniels* is a reminder of why this special connection between you and your spaniel exists—it is a collection of images and words that will cement in your mind for all of eternity an adoration for this hard-to-define-but-you-know-one-if-you've-got-one dog of all trades.

*Overleaf: The Welsh springer spaniel looks different than its cousin, the English springer spaniel, but both have little patience for photographers pursuing them during suppertime. Photograph © Kent and Donna Dannen*

# PART I

# Kids and Spaniels

*"The dog Nick was a red spaniel with long silky ears and a tail that never stopped wagging so long as he was with Adam. He had followed at Adam's heels since he was a round, wriggling ball of a puppy small enough to walk underneath the other dogs without stooping; he had slept with Adam—he was warm and soft to have in bed on cold nights—and had eaten some of whatever Adam had to eat; he was happy or tired or sad according as Adam was happy or tired or sad; his brown eyes were constantly on Adam's face and he went to great lengths to please his young god and master."*
—Elizabeth Janet Gray, *Adam of the Road,* 1942

Above: *Willing to put up with it but hardly thrilled about the situation, an English springer gets a whole new look.* Photograph © Ron Spomer
Left: *In an all-out cuteness battle, a blue-eyed baby and a button-nosed cocker puppy share a playpen.* Photograph © Kent and Donna Dannen

# The Coming of Number Three

## by Richard Burton

 Dogs and children are the peanut butter and jelly of animal-human relationships, and spaniels and kids bring this natural bond to another level. There is nothing more wonderful than to see a merry spaniel slobbering his adoration all over a resplendently happy child. And that same child will love that spaniel fiercely, as if the dog were a part of the boy or girl's soul.

Richard Burton's book *Three of a Kind* is a tale of just this kind of bond. First published in 1908, it is the story of a cocker spaniel and a newsboy, as well as an old musician, who loved the pup dearly.

Burton often wrote fondly of spaniels—and dogs of many other stripes—during his forty-year writing and academic career. A poet, English professor, biographer, editor, and journalist, Burton authored more than twenty books, including *Dumb in June* (1895), *From the Book of Life* (1909), *Bernard Shaw: The Man and the Mask* (1916), and *Higher Than Hills* (1937).

"The Coming of Number Three" is an excerpt from an early section of *Three of a Kind*. Here Burton employs wide literary brushstrokes to portray the initial meeting of the spaniel and the boy the dog quickly adopts.

*Unabashed happiness is evident in spaniels as well as kids.* Photograph © Daniel Dempster

THE COMING OF the dog Dun was in this wise. One day, in the bleak white of midwinter, Phil was standing at a particularly windswept corner, a cross-way of traffic where the sale of newspapers to home-returning toilers was keenest after five o'clock in the afternoon. He was crying in his clear treble and with the phonetics peculiar to his craft: "Here y're, Evenin' Post, Extry: Tribyune, all about the big fire: I-talian earthquake, five hundred swallowed up alive."

In the dream of world peace which to-day sets a few prescient souls aflame, I wonder if they include a kind of peace, less martial yet equally desirable: that which begins at home and means that our daily prints can be hawked with the same profit without raucous-voiced newsboys fouling the air with their cries of lust, murder and sudden disaster—just the sort of thing from which poor humanity would flee when it goes forth of a morning fresh from sleep and with hope at

*A springer spaniel puppy that would thrill any child.* Photograph © Judith E. Strom

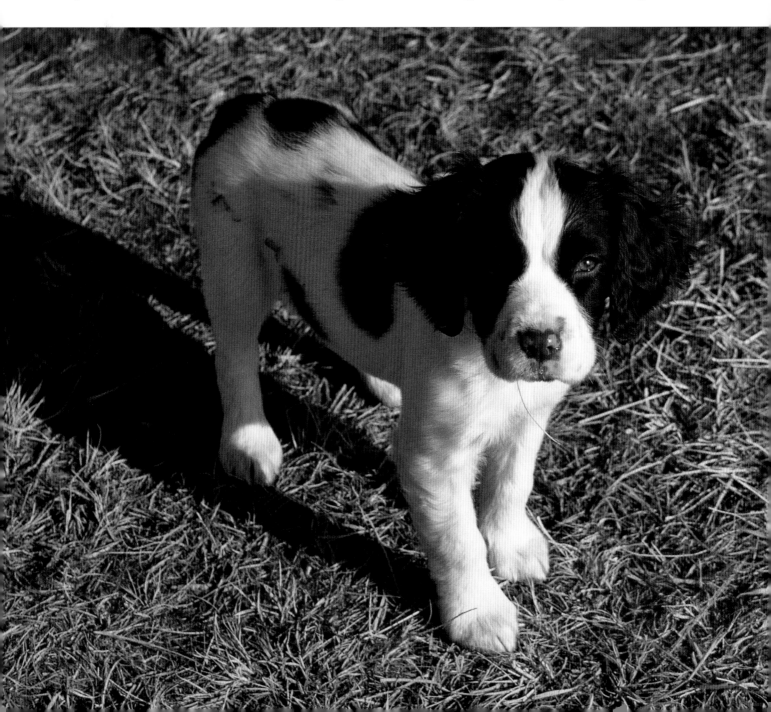

heart, or as it goes home to rest and take comfort after the strain of the working hours?

Think of the relief, the joy, of hearing such corner calls as these: "Here y're! Restoration of kidnapped boy! Just out! Special: Millionaire's gift to the blind! Big sensation: Honest thief in State's Prison! Extry: Hero saves a railroad train!" Really, when you stop to think of it, there are a lot of dramatic occurrences in a day, doings which are neither grim nor terrible: acts that encourage humanity in the triumphal march towards better things. Mayhap the day will come when we shall no longer be asked to breakfast with disaster and sup on horrors. Meanwhile, the yellow journal feeds itself fat on such food; which is where it differs from a yellow dog.

Suddenly, at Phil's feet stood a little animal looking up at him in utter friendliness, the eye a-yearn as only a dog's can, the tail supplementing the eye-speech with no less eloquence of love. It seemed a telepathic recognition, an unprecedented offer of brotherhood. The fine silky, black hair of the brute (how one hates to use the word where Love is), a cocker spaniel, by breed, was wofully bemired, his feathers drooped disconsolate. But his whole bearing was gay, not dejected: the very spirit of the light-foot comrade shone forth from his entire personality. Moreover, his points, although obscured by his present plight, were aristocratic for the knowing eye. So he stood gazing up at the lad, barking now and again to attract attention, if Phil's business cares took his eye from this new friend. It was as if the dog said in so many words: "I like you, I need you; make me yours and all will be well."

And it was evident that this appeal was not made piteously, but as man to man, because of an instant perception in the canine mind that here was a fellow after his own heart. In the big world of humans, these sudden likings are common enough. Some of us even believe in love at first sight,—or if we don't, our children do, and act accordingly, much to our alarm. Why then, forsooth, should we not allow the same privilege to animals, whose instincts take the place of our boasted reasoning faculties and not seldom make those faculties look slow and blundering? Half the romance of history begins thus, with the chance meeting of strangers at the cross-ways of Life.

There was nothing to mark ownership in the dog; no collar adorned his neck, nor were there signs of gentle care in his keeping. Yet, as we said, Nature had made him a beautiful creature: with his luxuriant soft thick coat, handsomely feathered, with the slender snout esteemed of fanciers, and with animation and ease in all his movements; and with the crowning gift and grace of rich brown eyes, which now, seeking Phil's, held a pleading that was well-nigh irresistible. Phil took him to be homeless, or lost, at any rate, in the devious paths of the city, in that section of it where ancient cowpaths and tortuous lanes have resulted in a down-town tangle, apt to confuse even the superior intellect of man.

This cocker had a way of looking up at you, head perked a little to one side, one ear drooping properly forward but the other turned coquettishly back, and with an arch, quizzical expression of countenance which had all the effect of a keen appreciation of the humors of life; and was potent to draw out affection in every one save those unfortunates condemned by an inscrutable fate to indifference toward man's best friend among brute kind. He took that pose now, and Phil was a ready victim. Young as he was, he could feel in a vague way the pathos of being a dumb outcast in a great city,—indeed, had not Phil himself been very much in the same boat? And his soul, all unknowingly, also responded to an exhibition of pluck in taking such a sorry lot debonnairely: Phil was not immune from the contagion of courage.

As trade slackened and the bunch of papers melted away, he pondered the proper action and made wrong change to his mortification several times, because of his absent-mindedness. The dog showed not the slightest intention of departure; it was plain he intended to stick to this self-elected master; he was the very figure of constancy in action. When, at last, the boy turned his face toward the lane that gave on the old graveyard, the canine trotted obediently after, unrepulsed, without so much as a whistle to bring him to heel. His carriage implied there had been a close relation between the two from time out of mind. Now and again he would bound ahead of the boy, looking back with the light of an expectant gratitude in those leal brown eyes. He seemed to rebuke the other for his slow progress. When he trotted more sedately just ahead of the boy (satisfied that the other would follow), there was something both appealing and comic in his gait. The forward movement of a small dog is for all the world like that of a side-paddle steamer going transverse to the current.

Yet Phil made short work of the mile between him and supper. Not only did hunger impel him, he had, too, the additional incentive of the surprise to the master. Truth to tell, his query was not unmingled with a mild alarm. He knew Ludovic liked animals of all sorts. Had he not one day, before Phil's very eyes, rescued a wretched gutter cat from the machinations of a gang of urchins who were striving to make a practical demonstration of the proverb which declares that animal to be possessed of nine lives: apparently meaning nine times the usual chance for torture? And in some of their suburban journeyings he had noticed the old musician's gentle delight in those merry little wights, the birds: a joy which might have reminded Phil of St. Francis of Assisi, had the former been a literary man instead of a newsboy whose handsome face was not always perfectly clean, and whose hands never were. Still, Ludovic might not take an immediate, violent fancy to the little black cocker, which already, by its frank and affectionate demeanour, was winning its way into Phil's too fond heart.

But the fears were groundless. As the twain entered the living room, after a stair-climb in which the dog boldly led the way, as if he, not the boy, were mine host, the animal rushed toward Ludovic, seated in his corner, with an assurance of kindly welcome no less pathetic

Facing page: *A young Irish water spaniel and a similarly young boy relax*. Photograph © Tara Darling

*An American cocker spaniel jogs through a field of tall grass.* Photograph © Daniel Dempster

than sublime. And the musician, after the first moment of amazement taking in the situation at once, made a mock heroic gesture of despair and exclaimed with a comical moue: "It is a hound, yes—and I am his long lost father, eh? And thou art his brother, Phil, nicht? See, he smells the stew.—He must eat yet, before he go!"

But of course he never went. The two comrades were an easy prey to the blandishments of the third, who by morning—for it would have been cruelty undreamt of to turn him out that night—had so ingratiated himself into their affections that they made excuses to each other for keeping him day by day; knowing all the while in their guilty hearts that he already belonged, as much as they themselves. Until finally, throwing aside all pretence, they shamelessly organized themselves into the trinity of the top floor.

His name had been a matter of some concern. You will have observed that Dun was not dun-colored. Nay, on the contrary, there was theatrical history in his cognomen. Phil, with the delicacy of a true gentleman, waived the right of discovery and insisted on Ludovic as the proper baptismal authority. Now, the musician had once played in an orchestra where he had witnessed the performance of the elder Sothern as Lord Dundreary,—one of the pleasant memories of the older theater goers of this land. He had laughed, as have most of us who are past forty, at the peculiar little skip which the actor introduced, at first by accident in a rehearsal, into the walk of the funny fop,—to the huge content of his audience. One day Ludovic observed that the dog, busily threading the way in front of them on a Sunday outing, feet a-twinkle, skipped a step with one of his hind legs; instantly, Sothern flashed upon his amused mind; the resemblance threw him into Jovian laughter. So then and there, *Dundreary* was the animal dubbed. And this, after the immemorial usage in respect of names, was reduced to Dun,—and accepted gratefully by all concerned.

And most kindly did Dun, now once and for all reclaimed from the ranks of the vagrants, take to his new life. There is in the cocker nature (as contrasted with other breeds) an extra share of the nomadic instinct, the *Wanderlust* of all free farers after joy. Hence, dearly he loved his days in the street. Even when masterless and unsure of his next meal, he had enjoyed them; but now, with fire and food and friends—another of the world's sweet trinities—to greet him at the day's end, his mood was beatific. What bliss unalloyed to dodge vehicles, bark up alleys, touch noses with stranger dogs, and always follow, follow, follow after at the beck of the Two, in the camaraderie of a common zest for life. Dogs when happy are perfectly happy: and even when things go against them, they assume the best and keep up a cheerful attitude towards life: they are the first Christian Scientists in history.

Two distinct duties were his: on the one hand, he would help Phil sell his papers—for within a month he was so trained that he surprised and delighted gaping crowds of folks at Phil's corner by his antics and was a source of much revenue to the newsboy. Or again, he would trot beside Ludovic through the residential avenues, perch near while the musician played and, tin cup in mouth, gather coppers when the music ceased: and during its production, do his full share toward the securing of orchestral effects.

This last statement is no mere trope of speech, for Dun literally assisted the musicians in their work; it is quite accurate to describe him as a musical dog. He always co-operated in the performance of the various selections. Seated close beside Ludovic, he would lift up his head, look languishingly to heaven, and emit sounds which, if they were not mellifluous, certainly implied emotion on his part, and moreover, were fully as efficacious in the bringing in of money, thrown from the windows or drawn from the pockets of passers-by, as were the concerted efforts of the remaining members of the band. Even as Orpheus lured wild animals to follow him by his sweet pipings, so did this tame animal lure human beings.

Sometimes, in his excitement, Dun would rise from his sitting posture and stand on his hind legs—the very attitude he was to assume later in the day when a vendor of newspapers in the service of Phil. This, however, was when the selection was of a particularly sad, lacrymosal sort. For it is to be remarked that the manner of Dun's singing—it could be called naught else—and his general deportment, varied according to the style of composition. Yes, he seemed susceptible not only to pitch, intensity and tempo, but to the more subjective and subtle elements which have to do with harmony, sentiment, theme. A brisk merry dance tune, running from violin to flute like a wind in a wheat field (this street band boasted both brass and wood wind instruments), would draw from him a succession of short, staccato yelps, as he lay on his belly with head erect: to a mournful, slow-moving melody he would respond by long-drawn-out plaintive whines, perhaps with head between his paws; while the crashing close harmonies of a composer like Wagner would bring him in a trice to his feet, tail and head pointing, the whole body tense and vibrant, and making noise enough to rival the music—almost.

To the uninstructed, this might seem like angry protest against the music of the future; but Ludovic knew, from many private experiments at home, that Dun was in truth a firm adherent of the Wagnerian school, a creature not to be scared off even by the extremes of a Richard Strauss. There is work yet to do, by the by, for our laboratory psychologists in the study of the musical sensitiveness of the lower orders of sentient beings.

Six months after Dun's adoption, he was as firmly lodged in the affections of his two friends as if he had been always by their side. All their plans and pleasures included him; and in return for such feeling the dog gave them a devotion which, this side of heaven, they were unlikely to receive again. For often in the unquestioning fealty of those we mis-call brutes, is to be found a not unworthy foreglimpse of that final love which, our best moments whisper, shall pilot this blundering old world to a safe haven at last: that spirit in whose loving kindness, as Dante has sung it, we are ever fain to find our peace.

Facing page: *It's suppertime for these two American cockers.* Photograph © Isabelle Francais
Overleaf: *Two American cocker puppies get a ride in a five-year-old girl's wagon on an autumn day.* Photograph © Alan and Sandy Carey

# The Dimmocks

## *by* James Herriot

 Born James Alfred Wight, the author to be known to the world as James Herriot worked as a country veterinarian in England until penning his first book, *If Only They Could Talk*, in 1970, when he was in his fifties. Adopting the Herriot pseudonym, the veterinarian-turned-author had no idea of the phenomenal success and international notoriety that this late-blooming choice of avocations would bring to him. After the publication in England of his second book, *It Shouldn't Happen to a Vet*, Herriot's first two books were released in the United States in one volume under the title *All Creatures Great and Small*. The book was an instant bestseller, and the life of the private, humble country veterinarian was never to be the same.

"The Dimmocks" is the story of a sick cocker loved dearly by a child. In treating the mysterious illness of the dog, Herriot chooses to consult his old friend Granville Bennett, a boisterous master veterinarian.

*A wary English cocker spaniel puppy sits in the sunshine.* Photograph © Kent and Donna Dannen

A FULL SURGERY! But the ripple of satisfaction as I surveyed the packed rows of heads waned quickly as realisation dawned. It was only the Dimmocks again.

I first encountered the Dimmocks one evening when I had a call to a dog which had been knocked down by a car. The address was down in the old part of the town and I was cruising slowly along the row of decaying cottages looking for the number when a door burst open and three shock-headed little children ran into the street and waved me down frantically.

"He's in ere, Mister!" they gasped in unison as I got out, and then began immediately to put me in the picture.

"It's Bonzo!" "Aye, a car 'it 'im!" "We 'ad to carry 'im in, Mister!" They all got their words in as I opened the garden gate and struggled up the path with the three of them hanging on to my arms and tugging at my coat; and en route I gazed in wonder at the window of the house where a mass of other young faces mouthed at me and a tangle of arms gesticulated.

Once through the door which opened directly into the living room I was swamped by a rush of bodies and borne over to the corner where I saw my patient.

Bonzo was sitting upright on a ragged blanket. He was a large

*Filled with curiosity, a Welsh springer spaniel pup checks out the family tortoise.* Photograph © Robert and Eunice Pearcy

shaggy animal of indeterminate breed and though at a glance there didn't seem to be much ailing him he wore a pathetic expression of self-pity. Since everybody was talking at once I decided to ignore them and carry out my examination. I worked my way over legs, pelvis, ribs and spine; no fractures. His mucous membranes were a good colour, there was no evidence of internal injury. In fact the only thing I could find was slight bruising over the left shoulder. Bonzo had sat like a statue as I felt over him, but as I finished he toppled over on to his side and lay looking up at me apologetically, his tail thumping on the blanket.

"You're a big soft dog, that's what you are," I said and the tail thumped faster.

I turned and viewed the throng and after a moment or two managed to pick out the parents. Mum was fighting her way to the front while at the rear, Dad, a diminutive figure, was beaming at me over the heads. I did at bit of shushing and when the babel died down I addressed myself to Mrs. Dimmock.

"I think he's been lucky," I said. "I can't find any serious injury. I think the car must have bowled him over and knocked the wind out of him for a minute, or he may have been suffering from shock."

The uproar broke out again. "Will 'e die, Mister?" "What's the matter with 'im?" "What are you going to do?"

I gave Bonzo an injection of a mild sedative while he lay rigid, a picture of canine suffering, with the tousled heads looking down at him with deep concern and innumerable little hands poking out and caressing him.

Mrs. Dimmock produced a basin of hot water and while I washed my hands I was able to make a rough assessment of the household. I counted eleven little Dimmocks from a boy in his early teens down to a grubby-faced infant crawling around the floor; and judging by the significant bulge in Mum's midriff the number was soon to be augmented. They were clad in a motley selection of hand-me-downs, darned pullovers, patched trousers, tattered dresses, yet the general atmosphere in the house was of unconfined *joie de vivre*.

Bonzo wasn't the only animal and I stared in disbelief as another biggish dog and a cat with two half-grown kittens appeared from among the crowding legs and feet. I would have thought that the problem of filling the human mouths would have been difficult enough without importing several animals.

But the Dimmocks didn't worry about such things; they did what they wanted to do, and they got by. Dad, I learned later, had never done any work within living memory. He had a "bad back" and lived what seemed to me a reasonably gracious life, roaming interestedly around the town by day and enjoying a quiet beer and a game of dominoes in a corner of the Four Horse Shoes by night.

I saw him quite often; he was easy to pick out because he invariably carried a walking stick which gave him an air of dignity and he always walked briskly and purposefully as though he were going somewhere important.

I took a final look at Bonzo, still stretched on the blanket, looking up at me with soulful eyes, then I struggled towards the door.

"I don't think there's anything to worry about," I shouted above the chattering which had speedily broken out again, "but I'll look in tomorrow and make sure."

When I drew up outside the house next morning I could see Bonzo lolloping around the garden with several of the children. They were passing a ball from one to the other and he was leaping ecstatically high in the air to try to intercept it.

He was clearly none the worse for his accident but when he saw me opening the gate his tail went down and he dropped almost to his knees and slunk into the house. The children received me rapturously.

"You've made 'im better, Mister!" "He's all right now, isn't he?" "He's 'ad a right big breakfast this mornin', Mister!"

I went inside with little hands clutching at my coat. Bonzo was sitting bolt upright on his blanket in the same attitude as the previous evening, but as I approached he slowly collapsed on to his side and lay looking up at me with a martyred expression.

I laughed as I knelt by him. "You're the original old soldier, Bonzo, but you can't fool me. I saw you out there."

I gently touched the bruised shoulder and the big dog tremblingly closed his eyes as he resigned himself to his fate. Then when I stood up and he realised he wasn't going to have another injection he leapt to his feet and bounded away into the garden.

There was a chorus of delighted cries from the Dimmocks and they turned and looked at me with undisguised admiration. Clearly they considered that I had plucked Bonzo from the jaws of death. Mr. Dimmock stepped forward from the mass.

"You'll send me a bill, won't you," he said, with the dignity that was peculiar to him.

My first glance last night had decided me that this was a no-charging job and I hadn't even written it in the book, but I nodded solemnly.

"Very well, Mr. Dimmock, I'll do that."

And throughout our long association, though no money ever changed hands, he always said the same thing—"You'll send me a bill, won't you."

This was the beginning of my close relationship with the Dimmocks. Obviously they had taken a fancy to me and wanted to see as much as possible of me. Over the succeeding weeks and months they brought in a varied selection of dogs, cats, budgies, rabbits at frequent intervals, and when they found that my services were free they stepped up the number of visits; and when one came they all came. I was anxiously

Facing page: *Kids and spaniel puppies were made for each other.* Photograph © Marilyn "Angel" Wynn

*Nothing is sadder than the eyes of an ill spaniel puppy, especially when the spaniel belongs to a child.* Photograph © Bryan and Cherry Alexander

trying to expand the small animal side of the practice and increasingly my hopes were raised momentarily then dashed when I opened the door and saw a packed waiting room.

And it increased the congestion when they started bringing their auntie, Mrs. Pounder, from down the road with them to see what a nice chap I was. Mrs. Pounder, a fat lady who always wore a greasy velour hat perched on an untidy mound of hair, evidently shared the family tendency to fertility and usually brought a few of her own ample brood with her.

That is how it was this particular morning. I swept the assembled company with my eye but could discern only beaming Dimmocks and Pounders; and this time I couldn't even pick out my patient. Then the assembly parted and spread out as though by a prearranged signal and I saw little Nellie Dimmock with a tiny puppy on her knee.

Nellie was my favourite. Mind you, I liked all the family; in fact they were such nice people that I always enjoyed their visits after that first disappointment. Mum and Dad were always courteous and cheerful and the children, though boisterous, were never ill-mannered; they were happy and friendly and if they saw me in the street they would wave madly and go on waving till I was out of sight. And I saw them often because they were continually scurrying around the town doing odd jobs—delivering milk or papers. Best of all, they loved their animals and were kind to them.

But as I say, Nellie was my favourite. She was about nine and had suffered an attack of "infantile paralysis," as it used to be called, when very young. It had left her with a pronounced limp and a frailty which set her apart from her robust brothers and sisters. Her painfully thin legs seemed almost too fragile to carry her around but above the pinched face her hair, the colour of ripe corn, flowed to her shoulders and her eyes, though slightly crossed, gazed out calm and limpid blue through steel-rimmed spectacles.

"What's that you've got, Nellie?" I asked.

"It's a little dog," she almost whispered. "'e's mine."

"You mean he's your very own?"

She nodded proudly. "Aye, 'e's mine."

"He doesn't belong to your brothers and sisters, too?"

"Naw, 'e's mine."

Rows of Dimmock and Pounder heads nodded in eager acquiescence as Nellie lifted the puppy to her cheek and looked up at me with a smile of a strange sweetness. It was a smile that always tugged at my heart; full of a child's artless happiness and trust but with something else which was poignant and maybe had to do with the way Nellie was.

"Well, he looks a fine dog to me," I said. "He's a Spaniel, isn't he?"

She ran a hand over the little head. "Aye, a Cocker. Mr. Brown said 'e was a Cocker."

There was a slight disturbance at the back and Mr. Dimmock appeared from the crush. He gave a respectful cough.

"He's a proper pure bred, Mr. Herriot," he said. "Mr. Brown from the bank's bitch had a litter and 'e gave this 'un to Nellie." He tucked his stick under his arm and pulled a long envelope from an inside pocket. He handed it to me with a flourish. "That's 'is pedigree."

I read it through and whistled softly. "He's a real blueblooded hound, all right, and I see he's got a big long name. Darrowby Tobias the Third. My word, that sounds great."

I looked down at the little girl again. "And what do *you* call him, Nellie?"

"Toby," she said softly. "I calls 'im Toby."

I laughed. "All right, then. What's the matter with Toby anyway? Why have you brought him?"

"He's been sick, Mr. Herriot." Mrs. Dimmock spoke from somewhere among the heads. "He can't keep nothin' down."

"Well I know what that'll be. Has he been wormed?"

"No, don't think so."

"I should think he just needs a pill," I said. "But bring him through and I'll have a look at him."

Other clients were usually content to send one representative through with their animals but the Dimmocks all had to come. I marched along with the

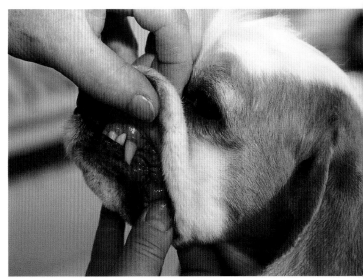

*An American cocker visits the vet.*
Photograph © Kent and Donna Dannen

crowd behind me filling the passage from wall to wall. Our consulting-cum-operating room was quite small and I watched with some apprehension as the procession filed in after me. But they all got in, Mrs. Pounder, her velour hat slightly askew, squeezing herself in with some difficulty at the rear.

My examination of the puppy took longer than usual as I had to fight my way to the thermometer on the trolley then struggle in the other direction to get the stethoscope from its hook on the wall. But I finished at last.

"Well I can't find anything wrong with him," I said. "So I'm pretty sure he just has a tummy full of worms. I'll give you a pill now and you must give it to him first thing tomorrow morning."

Like a football match turning out, the mass of people surged along the passage and into the street and another Dimmock visit had come to an end.

I forgot the incident immediately because there was nothing unusual about it. The pot-bellied appearance of the puppy made my diagnosis a formality; I didn't expect to see him again.

But I was wrong. A week later my surgery was once more overflowing and I had another squashed-in session with Toby in the little back room. My pill had evacuated a few worms but he was still vomiting, still distended.

"Are you giving him five very small meals a day as I told you?" I asked.

I received emphatic affirmatives and I believed them. The Dimmocks really took care of their animals. There was something else here, yet I couldn't find it. Temperature normal, lungs clear, abdomen negative on palpation; I couldn't make it out. I dispensed a bottle of our antacid mixture with a feeling of defeat. A young puppy like this shouldn't need such a thing.

This was the beginning of a frustrating period. There would be a span of two or three weeks when I would think the trouble had righted itself, then without warning the place would be full of Dimmocks and Pounders and I'd be back where I started.

And all the time Toby was growing thinner.

I tried everything: gastric sedatives, variations of diet, quack remedies. I interrogated the Dimmocks repeatedly about the character of the vomiting—how long after eating, what were the intervals between, and I received varying replies. Sometimes he brought his food straight back, at others he retained it for several hours. I got nowhere.

It must have been over eight weeks later—Toby would be about four months old—when I again viewed the assembled Dimmocks with a sinking heart. Their visits had become depressing affairs and I could not foresee anything better today as I opened the waiting-room door and allowed myself to be almost carried along the passage. This time it was Dad who was the last to wedge himself into the consulting room, then Nellie placed the little dog on the table.

I felt an inward lurch of sheer misery. Toby had grown despite his disability and was now a grim caricature of a Cocker Spaniel, the long silky ears drooping from an almost fleshless skull, the spindly legs pathetically feathered. I had thought Nellie was thin but her pet had outdone her. And he wasn't just thin, he was trembling slightly as he stood arch-backed on the smooth surface, and his face had the dull inward look of an animal which has lost interest.

The little girl ran her hand along the jutting ribs and the pale, squinting eyes looked up at me through the steel spectacles with that smile which pulled at me more painfully than ever before. She didn't seem worried. Probably she had no idea how things were, but whether she had or not I knew I'd never be able to tell her that her dog was slowly dying.

I rubbed my eyes wearily. "What has he had to eat today?"
Nellie answered herself. "He's 'ad some bread and milk."
"How long ago was that?" I asked, but before anybody could reply the little dog vomited, sending the half-digested stomach contents soaring in a graceful arc to land two feet away on the table.
I swung round on Mrs. Dimmock. "Does he always do it like that?"
"Aye, he mostly does—sends it flying out, like."
"But why didn't you tell me?"

*Still small enough to relax in a ceramic bowl, an American cocker spaniel puppy takes a little rest.*
Photograph © Norvia Behling

The poor lady looked flustered. "Well . . . I don't know . . . I . . ."

I held up a hand. "That's all right, Mrs. Dimmock, never mind." It occurred to me that all the way through my totally ineffectual treatment of this dog not a single Dimmock or Pounder had uttered a word of criticism so why should I start to complain now?

But I knew what Toby's trouble was now. At last, at long last, I knew.

And in case my present-day colleagues reading this may think I had been more than usually thick-headed in my handling of the case, I would like to offer in my defence that such limited text books as there were in those days made only a cursory reference to pyloric stenosis (narrowing of the exit of the stomach where it joins the small intestine) and if they did they said nothing about treatment.

But surely, I thought, somebody in England was ahead of the books. There must be people who were actually doing this operation . . . and if there were I had a feeling one might not be too far away . . .

I worked my way through the crush and trotted along the passage to the phone.

"Is that you, Granville?"

"*Jim!*" A bellow of pure unalloyed joy. "How are you, laddie?"

"Very well, how are you?"

"Ab-so-lutely tip top, old son! Never better!"

"Granville, I've got a four-month-old spaniel pup I'd like to bring through to you. It's got pyloric stenosis."

"Oh lovely!"

*A liver-and-white English springer spaniel.* Photograph © Ron Spomer

"I'm afraid the little thing's just about on its last legs—a bag of bones."

"Splendid, splendid!"

"This is because I've been mucking about for four weeks in ignorance."

"Fine, just fine!"

"And the owners are a very poor family. They can't pay anything, I'm afraid."

"Wonderful!"

I hesitated a moment. "Granville, you do . . . er . . . you have . . . operated on these cases before?"

"Did five yesterday."

"What!"

A deep rumble of laughter. "I do but jest, old son, but you needn't worry, I've done a few. And it isn't such a bad job."

"Well that's great." I looked at my watch. "It's half past nine now. I'll get Siegfried to take over my morning round and I'll see you before eleven."

Granville had been called out when I arrived and I hung around his surgery till I heard the expensive sound of the Bentley purring into the yard. Through the window I saw yet another magnificent pipe glinting behind the wheel, then my colleague, in an impeccable pin-striped suit which made him look like the Governor of the Bank of England, paced majestically towards the side door.

"Good to see you, Jim!" he exclaimed, wringing my hand warmly. Then before removing his jacket he took his pipe from his mouth and regarded it with a trace of anxiety for a second before giving it a polish with his yellow cloth and placing it tenderly in a drawer.

It wasn't long before I was under the lamp in the operating room bending over Toby's small outstretched form while Granville—the other Granville Bennett—worked with fierce concentration inside the abdomen of the little animal.

"You see the gross gastric dilatation," he murmured. "Classical lesion." He gripped the pylorus and poised his scalpel. "Now I'm going through the serous coat." A quick deft incision. "A bit of blunt dissection here for the muscle fibres . . . down . . . down . . . a little more . . . ah, there it is, can you see it—the mucosa bulging into the cleft. Yes . . . yes . . . just right. That's what you've got to arrive at."

I peered down at the tiny tube which had been the site of all Toby's troubles. "Is that all, then?"

"That's all, laddie." He stepped back with a grin. "The obstruction is relieved now and you can take bets that this little chap will start to put weight on now."

"That's wonderful, Granville. I'm really grateful."

"Nonsense, Jim, it was a pleasure. You can do the next one yourself now, eh?" He laughed, seized needle and sutures and sewed up the abdominal muscles and skin at an impossible pace.

A few minutes later he was in his office pulling on his jacket, then as he filled his pipe he turned to me.

"I've got a little plan for the rest of the morning, laddie."

I shrank away from him and threw up a protective hand. "Well now, er . . . it's kind of you, Granville, but I really . . . I honestly must get back . . . we're very busy, you know . . . can't leave Siegfried too long . . . work'll be piling up . . ." I stopped because I felt I was beginning to gibber.

My colleague looked wounded. "All I meant, old son, was that we want you to come to lunch. Zoe is expecting you."

"Oh . . . oh, I see. Well that's very kind. We're not going . . . anywhere else, then?"

"Anywhere else?" He blew out his cheeks and spread his arms wide. "Of course not. I just have to call in at my branch surgery on the way."

"Branch surgery? I didn't know you had one."

"Oh yes, just a stone's throw from my house." He put an arm round my shoulders. "Well let's go, shall we?"

As I lay back, cradled in the Bentley's luxury, I dwelt happily on the thought that at last I was going to meet Zoe Bennett when I was my normal self. She would learn this time that I wasn't a perpetually drunken oaf. In fact the next hour or two seemed full of rosy promise; an excellent lunch illumined by my witty conversation and polished manners, then back with Toby, magically resuscitated, to Darrowby.

I smiled to myself when I thought of Nellie's face when I told her her pet was going to be able to eat and grow strong and playful like any other pup. I was still smiling when the car pulled up on the outskirts of Granville's home village. I glanced idly through the window at a low stone building with leaded panes and a wooden sign dangling over the entrance. It read "Old Oak Tree Inn." I turned quickly to my companion.

"I thought we were going to your branch surgery?"

Granville gave me a smile of childish innocence. "Oh that's what I call this place. It's so near home and I transact quite a lot of business here." He patted my knee. "We'll just pop in for an appetiser, eh?"

"Now wait a minute," I stammered, gripping the sides of my seat tightly. "I just can't be late today. I'd much rather . . ."

Granville raised a hand. "Jim, laddie, we won't be in for long." He looked at his watch. "It's exactly twelve thirty and I promised Zoe we'd be home by one o'clock. She's cooking roast beef and Yorkshire pudding and it would take a braver man than me to let her pudding go flat. I guarantee we'll be in that house at one o'clock on the dot—O.K.?"

I hesitated. I couldn't come to much harm in half an hour. I climbed out of the car.

As we went into the pub a large man, who had been leaning on the counter, turned and exchanged enthusiastic greetings with my colleague.

"Albert!" cried Granville. "Meet Jim Herriot from Darrowby. Jim,

Facing page: *A spaniel—enthusiastic, happy, loyal—is a kid's best friend.* Photograph © Barbara von Hoffmann

this is Albert Wainright, the landlord of the Wagon and Horses over in Matherley. In fact he's the president of the Licensed Victuallers' Association this year, aren't you, Albert?"

The big man grinned and nodded and for a moment I felt overwhelmed by the two figures on either side of me. It was difficult to describe the hard, bulky tissue of Granville's construction but Mr. Wainright was unequivocally fat. A checked jacket hung open to display an enormous expanse of striped shirted abdomen overflowing the waistband of his trousers. Above a gay bow tie cheerful eyes twinkled at me from a red face and when he spoke his tone was rich and fruity. He embodied the rich ambience of the term "Licensed Victualler."

I began to sip at the half pint of beer I had ordered but when another appeared in two minutes I saw I was going to fall hopelessly behind and switched to the whiskies and sodas which the others were drinking. And my undoing was that both my companions appeared to have a standing account here; they downed their drinks, tapped softly on the counter and said, "Yes please, Jack," whereupon three more glasses appeared with magical speed. I never had a chance to buy a round. In fact no money ever changed hands.

It was a quiet, friendly little session with Albert and Granville carrying on a conversation of the utmost good humour punctuated by the almost soundless taps on the bar. And as I fought to keep up with the two virtuosos the taps came more and more frequently till I seemed to hear them every few seconds.

Granville was as good as his word. When it was nearly one o'clock he looked at his watch.

"Got to be off now, Albert. Zoe's expecting us right now."

And as the car rolled to a stop outside the house dead on time I realised with a dull despair that it had happened to me again. Within me a witch's brew was beginning to bubble, sending choking fumes into my brain. I felt terrible and I knew for sure I would get rapidly worse.

Granville, fresh and debonair as ever, leaped out and led me into the house.

"Zoe, my love!" he warbled, embracing his wife as she came through from the kitchen.

When she disengaged herself she came over to me. She was wearing a flowered apron which made her look if possible even more attractive.

"Hel-lo!" she cried and gave me that look which she shared with her husband as though meeting James Herriot was an unbelievable boon. "Lovely to see you again. I'll get lunch now." I replied with a foolish grin and she skipped away.

Flopping into an armchair I listened to Granville pouring steadily over at the sideboard. He put a glass in my hand and sat in another chair. Immediately the obese Staffordshire Terrier bounded on to his lap.

"Phoebles, my little pet!" he sang joyfully. "Daddykins is home again." And he pointed playfully at the tiny Yorkie who was sitting at his feet, baring her teeth repeatedly in a series of ecstatic smiles. "And I see you, my little Victoria, I see you!"

By the time I was ushered to the table I was like a man in a dream, moving sluggishly, speaking with slurred deliberation. Granville poised himself over a vast sirloin, stropped his knife briskly, then began to hack away ruthlessly. He was a prodigal server and piled about two pounds of meat on my plate, then he started on the Yorkshire puddings. Instead of a single big one, Zoe had made a large number of little round ones as the farmers' wives often did, delicious golden cups, crisply brown round the sides. Granville heaped about six of these by the side of the meat as I watched stupidly. Then Zoe passed me the gravy boat.

With an effort I took a careful grip on the handle, closed one eye and began to pour. For some reason I felt I had to fill up each of the little puddings with gravy and owlishly directed the stream into one then another till they were all overflowing. Once I missed and spilled a few drops of the fragrant liquid on the tablecloth. I looked up guiltily at Zoe and giggled.

*Loyalty is a hallmark of the spaniel breeds; get a spaniel, and you will always have a friend.* Photograph © Isabelle Francais

Zoe giggled back, and I had the impression that she felt that though I was a peculiar individual there was no harm in me. I just had this terrible weakness that I was never sober day or night, but I wasn't such a bad fellow at heart.

It usually took me a few days to recover from a visit to Granville and by the following Saturday I was convalescing nicely. It happened that I was in the market-place and saw a large concourse of people crossing

*Though relatively rare, Sussex spaniels are intelligent, loyal, tireless dogs once popular with farmers in southern England.*
Photograph © Judith E. Strom

the cobbles. At first I thought from the mixture of children and adults that it must be a school outing but on closer inspection I realised it was only the Dimmocks and Pounders going shopping.

When they saw me they diverted their course and I was engulfed by a human wave.

"Look at 'im now, Mister!" "He's eatin' like a 'oss now!" "He's goin' to get fat soon, Mister!" The delighted cries rang around me.

Nellie had Toby on a lead and as I bent over the little animal I could hardly believe how a few days had altered him. He was still skinny but the hopeless look had gone; he was perky, ready to play. It was just a matter of time now.

His little mistress ran her hand again and again over the smooth brown coat.

"You are proud of your little dog, aren't you, Nellie," I said, and the gentle squinting eyes turned on me.

"Yes, I am." She smiled that smile again. "Because 'e's mine."

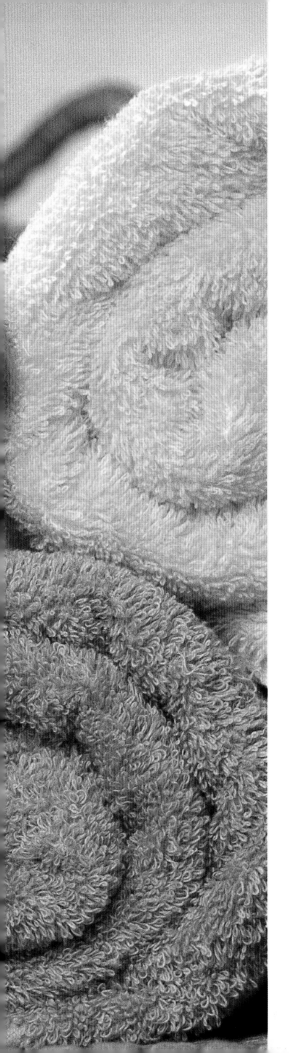

# PART II

# A Spaniel in our Midst

*"Spaniels as a rule are more inclined to be friendly to anyone and everyone than most other breeds of dogs . . . but most Spaniels are quite capable of entire devotion to one individual, if that individual deserves it. . . ."*
—C. A. Phillips and R. Claude Cane, *The Sporting Spaniel*, 1906

Above: *Those eyes of a spaniel! Is it any wonder why so many want a spaniel in their midst?* Photograph © Bryan and Cherry Alexander
Left: *Nine-weeks-old but low-key, an American cocker spaniel puppy lounges among rolled towels.* Photograph © Norvia Behling

# The Back Bedroom

## by Virginia Woolf

With a kind heart and a playful nature, a spaniel makes a glorious impact on the life of his family. What had once been a smooth-running, spaniel-free system becomes a jumbled chaos of kids and adults and fur. But the mayhem is filled with joy, because at its heart is a dog with a boundless capacity for love, devotion, and happiness.

In 1926, Virginia Woolf and her husband Leonard received a cocker spaniel as a gift from their friend Vita Sackville-West, and the dog did indeed have a glorious impact on their lives. In letters and diaries, Woolf wrote often of Pinka, as the cocker was called, and her antics.

Of course, Virginia Woolf was not only a spaniel lover but was also one of the leading writers of the twentieth century. Best-known for her provocative experimental works—many published by the Hogarth Press, which Leonard and Virginia Wolf founded in 1917—Woolf is the author of *The Voyage Out* (1915), *Jacob's Room* (1922), *Mrs. Dalloway* (1925), *To the Lighthouse* (1927), *Orlando* (1928), and *The Years* (1937), among others.

Pinka inspired Woolf to pen a largely fictional biography of Flush, poet Elizabeth Barrett's spaniel. "The Back Bedroom" is excerpted from *Flush: A Biography*, which was first published in 1933.

*Confined much of her time to her bedroom, Elizabeth Barrett was comforted by a cocker that refused to leave her side despite longing to be outdoors.* Photograph © Daniel Dempster

THE SUMMER OF 1842 was, historians tell us, not much different from other summers, yet to Flush it was so different that he must have doubted if the world itself were the same. It was a summer spent in a bedroom; a summer spent with Miss Barrett. It was a summer spent in London, spent in the heart of civilisation. At first he saw nothing but the bedroom and its furniture, but that alone was surprising enough. To identify, distinguish and call by their right names all the different articles he saw there was confusing enough. And he had scarcely accustomed himself to the tables, to the busts, to the washing-stands— the smell of eau de cologne still lacerated his nostrils, when there came one of those rare days which are fine but not windy, warm but not baking, dry but not dusty, when an invalid can take the air. The day came when Miss Barrett could safely risk the huge adventure of going shopping with her sister.

The carriage was ordered; Miss Barrett rose from her sofa; veiled and muffled, she descended the stairs. Flush of course went with her. He leapt into the carriage by her side. Couched on her lap, the whole pomp of London at its most splendid burst on his astonished eyes. They drove along Oxford Street. He saw houses made almost entirely of glass. He saw windows laced across with glittering streamers; heaped with

*A field spaniel puppy twosome relaxes.* Photograph © Isabelle Francais

gleaming mounds of pink, purple, yellow, rose. The carriage stopped. He entered mysterious arcades filmed with clouds and webs of tinted gauze. A million airs from China, from Arabia, wafted their frail incense into the remotest fibres of his senses. Swiftly over the counters flashed yards of gleaming silk; more darkly, more slowly rolled the ponderous bombazine. Scissors snipped; coins sparkled. Paper was folded; string tied. What with nodding plumes, waving streamers, tossing horses, yellow liveries, passing faces, leaping, dancing up, down, Flush, satiated with the multiplicity of his sensations, slept, drowsed, dreamt and knew no more until he was lifted out of the carriage and the door of Wimpole Street shut on him again.

And next day, as the fine weather continued, Miss Barrett ventured upon an even more daring exploit—she had herself drawn up Wimpole Street in a bath-chair. Again Flush went with her. For the first time he heard his nails click upon the hard paving-stones of London. For the first time the whole battery of a London street on a hot summer's day assaulted his nostrils. He smelt the swooning smells that lie in the gutters; the bitter smells that corrode iron railings; the fuming, heady smells that rise from basements—smells more complex, corrupt, violently contrasted and compounded than any he had smelt in the fields near Reading; smells that lay far beyond the range of the human nose; so that while the chair went on, he stopped, amazed; smelling, savouring, until a jerk at his collar dragged him on. And also, as he trotted up Wimpole Street behind Miss Barrett's chair he was dazed by the passage of human bodies. Petticoats swished at his head; trousers brushed his flanks; sometimes a wheel whizzed an inch from his nose; the wind of destruction roared in his ears and fanned the feathers of his paws as a van passed. Then he plunged in terror. Mercifully the chain tugged at his collar; Miss Barrett held him tight, or he would have rushed to destruction.

At last, with every nerve throbbing and every sense singing, he reached Regent's Park. And then when he saw once more, after years of absence it seemed, grass, flowers and trees, the old hunting cry of the fields hallooed in his ears and he dashed forward to run as he had run in the fields at home. But now a heavy weight jerked at his throat; he was thrown back on his haunches. Were there not trees and grass? he asked. Were these not the signals of freedom? Had he not always leapt forward directly Miss Mitford started on her walk? Why was he a prisoner here? He paused. Here, he observed, the flowers were massed far more thickly than at home; they stood, plant by plant, rigidly in narrow plots. The plots were intersected by hard black paths. Men in shiny top-hats marched ominously up and down the paths. At the sight of them he shuddered closer to the chair. He gladly accepted the protection of the chain. Thus before many of these walks were over a new conception had entered his brain. Setting one thing beside another, he had arrived at a conclusion. Where there are flower-beds there are asphalt paths; where there are flower-beds and asphalt paths, there

Overleaf: *A half dozen American cocker pups all in a row.* Photograph © Isabelle Francais

are men in shiny top-hats; where there are flower-beds and asphalt paths and men in shiny top-hats, dogs must be led on chains. Without being able to decipher a word of the placard at the Gate, he had learnt his lesson—in Regent's Park dogs must be led on chains.

And to this nucleus of knowledge, born from the strange experiences of the summer of 1842, soon adhered another: dogs, are not equal, but different. At Three Mile Cross Flush had mixed impartially with tap-room dogs and the Squire's greyhounds; he had known no difference between the tinker's dog and himself. Indeed it is probable that the mother of his child, though by courtesy called Spaniel, was nothing but a mongrel, eared in one way, tailed in another. But the dogs of London, Flush soon discovered, are strictly divided into different classes. Some are chained dogs; some run wild. Some take their airings in carriages and drink from purple jars; others are unkempt and uncollared and pick up a living in the gutter. Dogs therefore, Flush began to suspect, differ; some are high, others low; and his suspicions were confirmed by snatches of talk held in passing with the dogs of Wimpole Street. "See that scallywag? A mere mongrel! . . . By gad, that's a fine Spaniel. One of the best blood in Britain! . . . Pity his ears aren't a shade more curly. . . . There's a topknot for you!"

From such phrases, from the accent of praise or derision in which they were spoken, at the pillar-box or outside the public-house where the footmen were exchanging racing tips, Flush knew before the summer had passed that there is no equality among dogs: there are high dogs and low dogs. Which, then, was he? No sooner had Flush got home than he examined himself carefully in the looking-glass. Heaven be praised, he was a dog of birth and breeding! His head was smooth; his eyes were prominent but not gozzled; his feet were feathered; he was the equal of the best-bred cocker in Wimpole Street. He noted with approval the purple jar from which he drank—such are the privileges of rank; he bent his head quietly to have the chain fixed to his collar—such are its penalties. When about this time Miss Barrett observed him staring in the glass, she was mistaken. He was a philosopher, she thought, meditating the difference between appearance and reality. On the contrary, he was an aristocrat considering his points.

But the fine summer days were soon over; the autumn winds began to blow; and Miss Barrett settled down to a life of complete seclusion in her bedroom. Flush's life was also changed. His outdoor education was supplemented by that of the bedroom, and this, to a dog of Flush's temperament, was the most drastic that could have been invented. His only airings, and these were brief and perfunctory, were taken in the company of Wilson, Miss Barrett's maid. For the rest of the day he kept his station on the sofa at Miss Barrett's feet. All his natural instincts were thwarted and contradicted. When the autumn winds had blown last year in Berkshire he had run in wild scampering across the stubble; now at the sound of the ivy tapping on the pane Miss Barrett asked Wilson to see to the fastenings of the window. When the leaves of the

Facing page: *Elizabeth Barrett is far from the only famous person to keep a spaniel by their side. Everyone from Mary Queen of Scots and Sir Isaac Newton to Richard Nixon and Phyllis Diller shared some of their life with a spaniel.* Photograph © Bill Kinney

*Two cockers enjoy the summer sunshine.* Photograph © Daniel Dempster

scarlet runners and nasturtiums in the window-box yellowed and fell she drew her Indian shawl more closely round her. When the October rain lashed the window Wilson lit the fire and heaped up the coals. Autumn deepened into winter and the first fogs jaundiced the air. Wilson and Flush could scarcely grope their way to the pillar-box or to the chemist. When they came back, nothing could be seen in the room but the pale busts glimmering wanly on the tops of the wardrobes; the peasants and the castle had vanished on the blind; blank yellow filled the pane. Flush felt that he and Miss Barrett lived alone together in a cushioned and fire-lit cave. The traffic droned on perpetually outside with muffled reverberations; now and again a voice went calling hoarsely, "Old chairs and baskets to mend," down the street: sometimes there was a jangle of organ music, coming nearer and louder; going further and fading away. But none of these sounds meant freedom, or action, or exercise. The wind and the rain, the wild days of autumn and the cold days of mid-winter, all alike meant nothing to Flush except warmth and stillness; the lighting of lamps, the drawing of curtains and the poking of the fire.

At first the strain was too great to be borne. He could not help dancing round the room on a windy autumn day when the partridges must be scattering over the stubble. He thought he heard guns on the breeze. He could not help running to the door with his hackles raised when a dog barked outside. And yet when Miss Barrett called him back, when she laid her hand on his collar, he could not deny that another feeling, urgent, contradictory, disagreeable—he did not know what to call it or why he obeyed it—restrained him. He lay still at her feet. To resign, to control, to suppress the most violent instincts of his nature—that was the prime lesson of the bedroom school, and it was one of such portentous difficulty that many scholars have learnt Greek with less—many battles have been won that cost their generals not half such pain. But then, Miss Barrett was the teacher. Between them, Flush felt more and more strongly, as the weeks wore on, was a bond, an uncomfortable yet thrilling tightness; so that if his pleasure was her pain, then his pleasure was pleasure no longer but three parts pain. The truth of this was proved every day. Somebody opened the door and, whistled him to come. Why should he not go out? He longed for air and exercise; his limbs were cramped with lying on the sofa. He had never grown altogether used to the smell of eau de cologne. But no—though the door stood open, he would not leave Miss Barrett. He hesitated halfway to the door and then went back to the sofa. "Flushie," wrote Miss Barrett, "is my friend—my companion—and loves me better than he loves the sunshine without." She could not go out. She was chained to the sofa. "A bird in a cage would have as good a story," she wrote, as she had. And Flush, to whom the whole world was free, chose to forfeit all the smells of Wimpole Street in order to lie by her side.

*As ungainly as a human adolescent, a Welsh springer spaniel pup snoozes on a chair.* Photograph © Judith E. Strom

# A China Dog

## by C. Fred Bush
## (*Edited slightly by* Barbara Bush)

 C. Fred Bush—diplomat, friend of kings and movie stars, and quintessential Washington insider—had an illustrious career as the pet cocker spaniel of George and Barbara Bush. Born in 1973, just as George Bush rose to Chairman of the Republican National Committee, C. Fred trotted the globe from China to Washington to Houston to Kennebunkport and then back to Washington, when George Bush assumed the vice presidency in 1981. C. Fred died in 1987, before George Bush was elected president, and some might argue that "Freddy" was eventually eclipsed by the first dog Millie, an English springer spaniel sidekick of the Bushes while they occupied the White House. But such matters are beyond the scope of this book; we'll let the historians sort it out.

As tied as C. Fred was to the career trajectory of George Herbert Walker Bush, he was not the future president's dog; the cocker undeniably belonged to Barbara Bush. In fact, the dog was a birthday present to Mrs. Bush from her son Marvin. Mrs. Bush doted on Freddy, finding great joy and humor in her energetic spaniel. She even helped C. Fred write a book, *C. Fred's Story*, published in 1984, providing italicized commentary to Freddy's life story. The royalties from *C. Fred's Story* were donated by Barbara Bush to two national literacy organizations.

"A China Dog" from *C. Fred's Story* focuses on the mid-seventies when George Bush was appointed ambassador to China, and the Bushes packed up their household, including C. Fred, and moved to Peking.

*An English cocker spaniel on a pier by the sea.* Photograph © Sharon Eide/Elizabeth Flynn

IN THE SUMMER of 1974 Barbara was living in our gray house in Maine for the month of August. All the children were coming to visit us and George came for weekends. I could tell George was worried. One day Barbara got a phone call from George, who was in California, saying, "Why not meet me in D.C. tomorrow. Something's come up. I'm cutting my trip short and you ought to be with me." Something certainly did happen! The United States President resigned and our whole life changed. Bar left for Washington and when she came back George was with her. They gathered the children together and had them guess what job was next for George. Nobody guessed. Although nobody was more interested than I, I wasn't consulted. They kept talking about Peking and nobody mentioned me ever, not even once.

*Oh yes we did, and each time George said, "He can't go. They don't like dogs in China."*

We returned to Washington and one day Bar whispered to me, "Good news, Freddy. They have lots of diplomatic dogs in Peking." So she bought seventeen cases of dog food and sent them off to China with their other goods.

*At the time this seemed the only way to get George to agree. The investment in dog food was so big that we just couldn't afford not to take C. Fred with us. Incidentally, it was easier to get Freddy into China than any of our children or houseguests.*

Nobody prepared me for the trip to China. I, who slept with chairmen and chiefs, was put in a cage where I stayed for four days. I spent three of these days in quarantine in Japan while Barbara and George were having a glorious visit with the ambassador and his wife. Maybe this was to prepare me for what was to come later. There was certainly no freedom in China for me. I landed and was brought with the luggage to the United States Liaison Office. With the baggage! A man brought me to the house and opened the door of the cage. I heard Bar's voice, flew up the stairs, leapt into her arms and lathered her with kisses.

*And that's not all. My darling Freddy had a slight accident.*

I quickly found the perimeter of our property and where I could go and where I couldn't go. The latter was immense—all of China. The former was the walled compound where we had our house in one building and George's office in another. Between the two buildings was a fenced-in yard where I spent my days eating a bone or playing with a ball. I growled if someone came near my bone.

*Did he ever! George and I try to never get between C. Fred and a bone. He is such a grump.*

Some days when Bar was away and it was really cold outside, George let me go into the office. Everyone was nice to me; especially

Above: *An English cocker spaniel in a purple field of flowers.* Photograph © Barbara von Hoffmann
Facing page: *An English springer spaniel, much like C. Fred's successor, Millie, pants after a walk.* Photograph © Daniel Dempster
Overleaf: *A shaved American cocker spaniel pauses in the snow for photographs.* Photograph © Marilyn "Angel" Wynn

the United States security guards. They let me go on the rounds with them.

Outside of our compound gate stood two guards, members of the People's Liberation Army. For fourteen months I tried in vain to get them to look at me.

Inside the house there were some Chinese people to help us: a Mr. Sung and his helper, a Mrs. Chien, a Mrs. Wang, a Mr. Wang and a Mr. Chien.

*That may seem confusing. In China there are only about two hundred surnames. Many people have the same names. These Wangs and Chiens were not related.*

I teased Mrs. Chien and Mrs. Wang just like I teased Paula at home. I often stole their dustcloths and made them chase me. At first they were afraid of me and Bar was afraid that I was going to cause an international incident. In fact, all the Chinese were afraid of me at first, so each time new people came to work in the house, Bar would have me do all my tricks. When nobody was around, the Chinese patted me. I liked them. Needless to say, when George had official Chinese come to visit, I was banished to an upstairs bedroom. One of my favorite Chinese friends was Mrs. Tang, George and Bar's Chinese teacher. She came every day at noon and taught them nice things to say in Chinese. I always sat in on the lessons.

*In 1952 the Chinese had systematically searched out and killed all dogs. They were scavengers and thieves, roaming the streets in packs, sick with rabies. So the Chinese, who had loved dogs in the "bad old days," were taught that dogs were dangerous, dirty and, a bigger threat, they ate food that the starving population needed.*

Every morning when we lived in China, Bar or George walked me around the compound before breakfast. Sometimes I tried to make a break for the street to chase a wagon drawn by two donkeys and a skinny little horse or some other such interesting vehicle. I was always caught and brought back.

George and Bar explored Peking on their bikes. I was so jealous and wished I was back in Maine. Sometimes Bar put a long rope on my harness and rode up and down the street with me by her side. She didn't stay out too long because the crowds gathered.

Bar hit tennis balls to me in the driveway, being careful to keep the balls inside the compound. George, on the other hand, hit balls to me in the driveway, being careful to hit them outside the compound into the street to attract the schoolchildren walking back to school. Bar had me do my tricks so the children could see me. Without warning she stopped doing this and I missed seeing the children peek in the gate.

*The People's Liberation Army guards scolded the children and made them move on. So of course I stopped encouraging them, as I didn't want to cause them any pain.*

I had more baths in China. Bar says that I am honey-colored, but in China I was a gray. The pollution was so bad you could see the gray

Facing page: *Once you've seen the eyes of a spaniel, you are helpless under their power.* Photograph © William H. Mullins

*C. Fred was a friend of kings and presidents, as have been many Cavalier King Charles spaniels. Named for Charles II (King of England from 1660–1685), Cavalier King Charles spaniels are allowed in any public space in Britain, including the Houses of Parliament, a decree put on the books some 350 years ago by their namesake king.* Photograph © Sharon Eide/Elizabeth Flynn

climbing up my legs and in twenty-four hours I was gray again.

*As previously mentioned, we did sleep with Fred at our feet and therefore a clean C. Fred was much to be desired, especially as he inched up toward the pillow as the night drew on.*

One day in May of 1975 the Chinese announced that there would be no more hot water for three weeks. It was annual clean-the-hot-water-pipes-spring-cleaning-time. They heat the water centrally in China, which means it is heated in a centrally located place downtown. No more baths for me for three weeks while the Chinese blew the dirt from the pipes. I went from gray to grayer.

*Not only is the water heated centrally in Peking, but so are the houses. All the heat comes from burning coal and charcoal, thus the pollution.*

I met several dogs in China, including a large black Canadian poodle and a funny little terrier named Bubbles, who belonged to an American married to a German reporter. Bar liked Bubbles's family very much. I did not like Bubbles at all. I missed Amos.

We had lots of houseguests and Bar put a sign in their rooms.

*Beware of the Bush Dragon. He eats socks, furs, gloves and slippers. Please keep your doors closed or put your things up high. His name is C. Fred.*

This was a great challenge to me and there were very few guests who escaped. I especially liked one guest who wore cashmere socks. He told Bar that I could unpack locked suitcases. But my very favorite was Mrs. Hamon from Dallas, Texas. The day they were leaving she left

her fur coat and hat on her bed and went to have a last cup of coffee with George. The coat was too big, but the hat was just right. I had a nice chew and then pranced into the living room to show one and all. Usually I have trouble getting anyone to chase and play with me. This time Mr. and Mrs. Hamon joined in the game. I was in heaven, all four adults playing with me at one time. I liked Mrs. Hamon. She brushed up the fur and claimed that the hole that was there, wasn't.

*It was touch and go for Fred that day and he does owe Mrs. Hamon a big thank-you.*

Once when George took Barbara on a trip Jennifer Fitzgerald dog-sat with me. I moved right into her apartment. One night Jennifer was having a date. She rushed me home, gave me dinner and then ran in to bathe and change for her evening out. As she and her date were just relaxing with a drink, I thought a little game would be fun and came prancing into the living room with her panty hose hanging out of my mouth. This was greeted by a deep silence and there was no chase. Jennifer laughed. I liked Jennifer.

Jennifer also took me to the Great Wall of China, started in 500 B.C. and completed around 221 B.C. This wall meanders some fifteen hundred miles across the northern part of China. Bar and George didn't dare let me walk on the wall. Jennifer did, but even she winced when I performed on the Great Wall of China. I don't know why. After all, it was outdoors. Sometimes I don't understand people.

On the way home from the Great Wall we always stopped for a picnic lunch at the Ming tombs. The approach to the Ming tombs was guarded by the famous Avenue of the Animals, twelve stone animals on each side, twenty-four in all. Some of these seated and standing animals were real and some were mythical. Our guests always wanted to stop for pictures. Bar often put me on a rope and walked ahead with me up this marvelous sacred way, past the stone animals, the stone human statues and through gigantic red gates. All the time the commune members eyed me with great interest.

*The Chinese do have dogs in the country, but all these dogs run to a hound look. All "sleeve" dogs were killed because they represented decadence and the bad old days. A "sleeve" dog was a dog who fitted into a mandarin sleeve like a Pekingese, a Lhasa apso or a Shih Tzu.*

I loved the Ming tombs. This was the only place I could really run free. There are thirteen tombs about one half mile apart in a lovely valley. There are two big tourist tombs: the excavated tomb of Wan Li, the Porcelain Emperor, and the tomb of Yong Le, the second Ming Emperor. I couldn't go there because the Chinese didn't like dogs, and after being surrounded daily by a fourth of the world's population, I didn't like people!

*It was to those tombs that the Chinese and their foreign tourist friends went because that's where the buses went. No Chinese own their own cars. Every car in China is owned by the government with the exception of the diplomats' cars. Diplomats needed permission to travel anywhere outside the*

Facing page: *An American cocker spaniel puppy works its teeth on a rawhide bone.* Photograph © Norvia Behling

*twenty-mile limit except the Great Wall and the Ming tombs.*

My favorite tomb was the De Ling, the tomb of the Carpenter Emperor, T'ien Ch'i, who was very minor. This was a crumbly old tomb surrounded by a faded red wall topped with green and gold tiles. It was peaceful and quiet and Bar and guests ate on the old altar under several-hundred-year-old white pines and other evergreens while I ran and sniffed, begged food and chased imaginary dragons and phoenixes over broken altar pieces, cracked tiles, shards and through the tall grasses. Once when we arrived at the De Ling we found a herd of goats eating away and we retreated to another tomb that day. Bar and the houseguests explored the tomb, looked at the stele that rose out of the turtle's back and talked of times past while I ran and explored.

*I remember the day well. That was the first day that I realized that we were being observed. No sooner had we arrived than a man on a motorbike appeared, and it suddenly occurred to me that I had seen him on each visit. I came to look for him and he never failed me.*

As I implied earlier, we had wall-to-wall houseguests and we also had three visits from Dr. Henry Kissinger and one from President Ford. I was excluded from the Ford visit, but I was very much included in the first Kissinger visit. Dr. Kissinger, his wife, Nancy, and two children came for Thanksgiving lunch in 1974. It was a very quiet time, just family. I was invited in and Dr. Kissinger allowed as how he liked me. I liked him because he fed me candied Chinese nuts, one for him and one for me. I later heard George teasing Bar: "How come you let Henry feed Fred between meals when you won't let me?"

Andy came to visit once, but without Amos!

Every evening, no matter what the time or weather, Bar took me for a walk outside the gates before bedtime. We took a twenty-minute walk. Often a houseguest would come with us. George could rarely be persuaded to come with us, as he really only enjoys active competitive sports. We walked in the dark streets with the almost silent swishing of some of the four million bicycles in Peking going by, taking people to and from work. We took the same walk every night, past the Temple of the Sun Park, by the embassies—the British, the North Vietnamese, the Egyptian, the Rumanian, the Cuban and the Polish. I chased the Polish cat every night. I was on a long, long rope and never caught him.

One day George had been persuaded to take a walk with us. Suddenly he realized that people were looking at me with wonder in their eyes. He said in Chinese, *"Ta shi shau go* [He's a little dog]." Then all the Chinese said, "Oh, he's a little dog. He's not a cat." Not a cat! What a blow. Frankly I had thought that the Chinese connected me in someway with their great hero Chairman Mao. I often noticed that they said *mao* when they saw me. It turned out that *mao* said one way means "Chairman Mao" and another means "cat," my bitterest enemy!

*Many young Chinese had never seen a curly, long-haired dog. In his early days Freddy was more of a hippy type. Most people thought him quite feminine and would say, "Isn't she pretty?" For heaven's sake, don't tell C. Fred.*

*A wary cocker puppy.* Photograph © Kent and Donna Dannen

Bar learned to greet the Chinese with *"Ni bu pa. Ta shi shau go. Ta bu yau ren.* [Don't be afraid. He's a little dog. He doesn't bite people]." We made more friends.

I loved going for walks with George. He always gave me more rope and even let me off to chase the Polish cat. When George got to the last corner before our compound gate he would let me off the leash and we'd race to the house. One night when I was walking alone with Bar, we got to the corner and she let me off the leash. I raced away, but not to our house. I raced right across the street, past the PLA guards, up the steps and into the embassy of our neighbors from Gabon. This is how I went to my first dance. The chargé from Gabon was having an African dance and the music was too much for me to resist. Bar charged in after me and had to march the length of the dance floor to where I stood laughing at the end of the ballroom.

*Absolutely right. He was laughing and I could have killed him.*

Bar and George went to the Fur Fair and came home and said, "Some good news and some bad news, Freddy. The good news is that we saw a beautiful coat made of cat." Before I had time to enjoy this

Above: *The elongated Sussex spaniel is a wonderful friend.* Photograph © Kent and Donna Dannen
Facing page: *Oversize paws and all, an American cocker spaniel puppy poses for a portrait.* Photograph © Sharon Eide/Elizabeth Flynn
Overleaf: *Nosing each other aside to get to the good stuff, two American cocker puppies chow down.* Photograph © Sharon Eide/Elizabeth Flynn

amusing tidbit, they told me the bad news. They had also seen a blond coat made of dog fur. So I, with my beautiful buff, blond, honey-colored coat, always felt just a little threatened after that.

Shortly before we were to leave China the Chinese officials served dog at the Great Hall of the People and our Arab friends were insulted because they think dog is dirty. So what's with people? They wear dog, eat dog and think it's dirty?

Another time George came home from a banquet and could hardly meet my eye. He had been served and had eaten "upper lip of wild dog," after which he'd been told what it was. From then on until we left I could never tell if the Chinese liked me for me alone or as a potential coat or little dog stew. So in December of 1975 when we left, I left with some regret and much relief!

# PART III

# Days Afield

*"On a rug near my desk lies a sturdy, ten-year-old royally bred English springer spaniel, dear to me for his stout heart, faith in me, and an absorbing devotion to the gun. Only yesterday, as the first dampness touched the lowland bottoms with its chill of impending frost and gaudy colorings, Chub trod water in midstream of a swift river and barked for me to continue tossing sticks for him to fetch. After swimming ashore, he jumped a rabbit in the brush, and later treed a squirrel. Then, en route to our car, he nosed two bevies of bobwhites from corn and soybean coverts. Dead or alive, Chub brings home the bacon if it is loose at both ends."*
—Nash Buckingham, *Tattered Coat*, 1944

Above: *Soaking wet but having the time of his life, an English springer is ready to hunt.* Photograph © Sharon Eide/Elizabeth Flynn
Left: *Almost all of the spaniels were originally bred for the hunt. Today, English springer spaniels, like this pair in the western United States, and Welsh springer spaniels are the main hunting spaniels, though some of the others also capably go afield.* Photograph © Alan and Sandy Carey

# The Orphan

## *by* Paul A. Curtis

 Spaniels, like so many dog breeds, were originally hunting dogs, and many spaniels go afield to this day. Though Irish water spaniels and American water spaniels are considered retrievers, the other hunting spaniels—the English springer spaniel, Welsh springer spaniel, American cocker spaniel, English cocker spaniel, Clumber spaniel, field spaniel, and the Sussex spaniel—are specialists at flushing game; they force the gamebird into the air from its covey for the hunter to take down with his or her shotgun. Like their water spaniel brethren, they will then, in theory, retrieve the game.

Paul A. Curtis sought birds with numerous canine sidekicks during his long career as a shooting expert, editor, and author. Curtis served as the shooting editor for *Field & Stream* for fifteen years and later served as the editor of the magazines *Game* and *National Sportsman*. He contributed countless hunting sketches to the sporting magazines of his day, and penned seven books on hunting, including the *Outdoorsman's Handbook* (1920), *American Game Shooting* (1927), and *The Highlander* (1937).

"The Orphan" originally appeared in Curtis's 1938 book *Sportsmen All.*

*A beautiful Welsh springer spaniel.* Photograph © Judith E. Strom

BUSY WAS A black and white Welsh springer, a smallish bitch for her breed, with a muzzle some would have called a shade too pointed for the bench—but she was never doomed to that—thank God! Busy was born to the coverts and the bracken-covered hillsides from which it was her job to push all and sundry fur or feathers towards the gun. She had a fine high dome, and long sleeky ears which were always full of burrs, and a great pair of wide-set eyes, which Will Gladwin said were as dark as a sloe. I never knew what a sloe was, except the variety used for making gin, but anyway it was meant as a compliment, for Will had no more use for a light-eyed dog than I had—and it was his business to know.

Busy was imported from Wales by a great English trainer to run in the spaniel trials at Fishers Island, where I happened to be one of the guns. Naturally I did not take much notice of a novice in that galaxy of the springer constellation. Also I had enough to think about most of the time in bringing down pheasants for them to retrieve.

But a wise old sportsman, who has forgotten more about guns and gun dogs than most of us ever learn, had his kindly eyes upon her. And when she made a faultless exhibition performance with one of her running mates after the trial was over, under the command of that great handler William Humphries, to show how it really should be done, he made his offer and became her master for a sum which would have bought quite a lot of good gun dogs.

So Horsford Busy, who had a pedigree in which five British bench champions and eight field champions appeared in the six generations preceding her whelping, became the property of Mr. Louis Thebaud, and thereupon hangs my tale.

For many years I had sought woodcock through the hills of New Jersey with a nephew of Uncle Louis, as we fondly called him—and never did I accept an invitation to shoot with such alacrity as when I knew that grand old sportsman would be of the party.

Known, respected and loved, from the grouse moors of Scotland to the Susquehanna Flats and such intermediate stops as Monte Carlo—a crack shot, a rare host, a fascinating raconteur and, what is even rarer, a man of wealth overflowing with the milk of human kindness. One who loved his fellow men despite their frailties, loved them just a little better than he did a good gun dog, and could pick one or the other from the crowd with equal certainty, saying, "Here is a dog, and here is a man"—such was Uncle Louis.

One evening I had a call from my pal Chip Thebaud, asking me to come out to Morristown the following morning for a day's shooting, and I of course accepted. I remember that it was bitterly cold when I left the house in the grey dawn, to drive the eighty miles in an open speedster. One of those crisp December days when the air is as exhilarating as champagne—and scuds of white froth race across the deep blue sky.

Arriving at the familiar red house I got out stiffly and greeted the

Facing page: *The tireless nature of the Welsh springer spaniel—even a young one—makes it an excellent gun dog.* Photograph © Isabelle Francais

*The Welsh springer spaniel dates back at least to 1300, when an ancestor of the breed was mentioned in the* Laws of Wales. *Photograph © Marilyn "Angel" Wynn*

family who awaited me. Mendham had become a second home since the passing of my father. The elderly gentlemen—Chip's father Uncle Ed, and his tall brother Louis—drew me to the hearth, and a cup of steaming coffee soon put me right for the fray. Strangely enough both of these inseparable brothers were sorely afflicted. Uncle Ed was born with a withered arm, despite which he was Master of the Morris County Fox Hounds for many years, while Uncle Louis had lost an eye in a shooting accident at a time of life when most men lay away their guns—yet he still carried on.

Usually these greybeards went off together as they had done throughout life—while we comparative youngsters shot in another direction, and great was the rivalry between us. But Uncle Ed was failing fast in his last winter and was staying in, so it was agreed that we should have the treat of shooting with his brother.

At the kennels we picked up a brace of white and liver pointers—that dashed about and flung themselves against us in a wild abandon of delight at the prospects, and in their wake tumbled out a little springer who rushed up to me as if seeking someone, and then backed away. She went in turn to Uncle Louis, from whom she received a friendly pat, and then to Chip who paid no attention to her. As I watched her she stood back as if uncertain of herself, tail wagging and head cocked on one side in a troubled sort of way. She seemed to be waiting for a word of command, for someone to take notice of her and tell her what to do—yet no one did. It flashed across my mind that the little beastie was rather out of it in Mendham, in a family who were so pointer conscious.

"Isn't that the little springer you picked up at Fishers ?" I asked, turning to Uncle Louis. "How is she doing?"

"Yes," he replied with a half-sigh, "that's her—she hasn't found herself yet. Never will here, I am afraid. But," he added with a friendly nod in Chip's direction, "some people will never learn. Poor little doggie—America is very strange and wanting in game to you, isn't it?"

The spaniel threw him an appreciative look and promptly fell in at his heels, obviously thankful that someone had deigned to take notice of her, to whom she could attach herself. As we passed the barns a broad stretch of low swamp stretched before us in the valley and I observed with thanks—knowing it of old—that it was frozen hard.

The pointers capered about in front of us, getting rid of an excess of energy and the little spaniel watched them, tail awag, as if to say— "How I wish I could do that, too, but I should probably be well strapped if I presumed." Her coat was dull and lacking the sheen of the healthy spaniel, and she was thin as a herring—probably out of condition, I thought—it takes time for them to adjust themselves. Then we reached the margin of the swamp and our guns were loaded.

In a few moments the pointers were working upwind on a wily old Chinaman who was leading them a most circuitous course through the niggerheads. First one would point with the other backing and then the position would be reversed. With Uncle Louis in the center we advanced on the flanks waiting for the flush which never came.

Meanwhile the springer was working industriously in our rear, her stub of a tail going like mad to the accompaniment of most soul-satisfying sniffs of the aroma of pheasant.

"That spaniel seems to be getting hot," I observed, as she was drawing out of range.

"Oh, yes," answered Uncle Louis, in gentle sarcasm directed at Chip, "but we never pay any attention to her—apparently it's not the thing to do in Jersey—we just ignore her, you know."

"Nonsense," said Chip. "She hasn't got them. They are running ahead of the pointers and will do until we get to the end of the covert. Besides that little fool is backtracking them down wind."

Working down wind she was, and making a good job of it, too. I knew by her action that she had something in front of her and was getting close to it. Suddenly with a loud cackle a fine old cock went up from under her nose and not a gun within a hundred and fifty yards, while the staunch little dog sat down, marking it until out of sight, and then took up her quest again with many a backward look at us, wondering no doubt what those blasted Yanks went shooting for anyway. Uncle Louis looked at me and winked. Then we took on after the silent Chip and his pointers. And at that moment two more pheasants went into the air in front of the springer.

"Oh, hell!" I exploded.

"Yes, exactly," said Uncle Louis. "I'll admit it's a bit trying. Still in the course of time one may learn."

We whistled the spaniel in and went on over a low hill and down into the valley on the other side, and in an open meadow the old pointer stood with his running mate backing in beautiful style. The springer was ranging ahead, but noting that the others had stopped, she froze in her tracks. Score two for the springer—I said to myself—that was something new in spaniels to me; incidentally Busy was the only one I ever shot over with comfort when using pointers or setters, because she did not have to be kept at heel. One could always depend upon her to stand like a rock and honor a pointing dog.

We killed that bird and the springer brought it promptly to hand, and in the very next swamp she hustled two more birds into the air, which no one got a shot at because Chip insisted as usual that his precious pointers were right, and no one was on hand to shoot over her. We went home with the single bird between us to eat a disgruntled lunch.

Afterwards I made the announcement that whatever the others were doing I was going to tie to the spaniel for the afternoon.

"Why?" asked Chip. "Just because she was lucky this morning?"

"No," I said, "but because I like to shoot over a dog with which I can fire at anything, without shattering a tradition in a country where shots are so far between. Furthermore, it is my firm conviction, borne out by a lot of field-trial shooting, that a pheasant is not fair game for a pointer or setter. There are too many false points to suit me, and when one gets up, it is too easy. Me for the spaniel that hustles them into the air."

*An English cocker spaniel quarters—sweeps back and forth continuously—in order to flush game.* Photograph © Judith E. Strom

"That," murmured Uncle Louis, "is the theory upon which I purchased Busy. But you see how it is," and he expressively raised his shoulders. "I would suggest that you go around the base of the big hill with her this afternoon; most of the birds seem up in the fields at present. Unfortunately my legs are getting stiff for spaniel work, so I will go with Chip and the pointers. We should meet you before sundown on the other side and we can come home together—and we shall see what we shall see."

Off we started, the little springer industriously hunting before me. Once in a while she would turn to see if I was coming, never once did she range beyond gunshot. Just as a vivid streak of crimson which had been the setting sun showed over the ominous sable shadows of the woods in the valleys below me, I heard a shout and saw Uncle Louis and Chip approaching. I had three pheasants and two woodcock, they had a pheasant shared between them. The springer had scored again.

When we reached the summit of the hill on a short cut towards home, the light was still fairly good. I saw the white scut of a rabbit dart to a briar patch; the pointers were still ranging well ahead, so I cut loose and a red flame obscured my vision.

"Missed him," chuckled Uncle Louis. "Generally do in a poor light—shoot over the top of 'em."

But the spaniel had the case in hand, and dashing around the briars intercepted the rabbit on its way through the other side, and came up to me with the struggling little creature in her mouth.

"Now, there you are, Paul," chuckled Uncle Louis. "There is the dog for you—don't have to shoot at 'em—she catches 'em, and saves you all the embarrassment. Ought to get yourself one."

"I wish I owned this one," I answered ruefully.

"Well, my boy, you do. Take her home with you. Yes, I mean it—no one about here will do her justice. I spoiled this family of mine with the finest pointers and setters that money will buy, and they cannot see anything else. There is just one proviso goes with her—if you tire of her, destroy her; you must promise me that. I reserve the right to give away my dogs to those I know will treat them right, but I will not trust anyone else's judgment about it. They must not be given away again."

Give her away!

I would have given away my right arm more readily. Little Busy went home that night in my car—between us we taught my boy to shoot, and I was still killing game over her in her fourteenth year, when she was a fat old lady. The only way she ever embarrassed me was by taking other people's birds—anything that she could get hold of belonged to us. One time we were attending a great pheasant drive, and in a hot corner when I was firing like mad with Gladwin loading my second gun, Busy was busy collecting the kill. When the excitement was over the gentleman in the next stand, who had not secured such good shooting and had had time to watch me, came over and said, "No wonder you have such a good bag, Curtis. When that retriever of yours

Facing page: *A much needed water break after a hard day afield.*
Photograph © Isabelle Francais

*Pointer people may not think much of the spaniel clans, but spaniel people know springers were born for days afield.*
Photograph © Ron Spomer

collected all of your birds, she came over and took five of mine from under my very nose— would you consider selling her?" She had retrieved everything from snipe to geese for me before we put her away, and a month before that, when quite deaf and almost blind with cataract, she was in a dingle back of the kennels every day puttering about on a bevy of quail that must have known her well.

Strange things happen at times, and William Gladwin, the little Welshman who broke her to the gun and nursed her through distemper in the old country from which they both sprang, was the man who eventually put her in the ground. It seems fitting to me that it was so, for she had never forgotten him and loved him with all her staunch little heart. May the destiny which shapes our ends bless her with many rabbits to chase about in that Valhalla where I know that all good dogs must go.

# The Heart of My Hunting

## by Charles Fergus

 The English springer spaniel is the classic hunting spaniel; the very name of this spaniel belies the breed's hunting soul, as the dogs were once used to "spring" game into hunters' nets. This beautiful dog, with drooping ears, feathered coat, and lively tail, is at home during the chase.

Charles Fergus, a Pennsylvania-based freelance writer, shares his home with a springer and has often written about the breed in his articles and books. A frequent contributor to magazines such as *Shooting Sportsman* and *Sporting Classics*, Fergus has also written several books about hunting, including *A Rough-Shooting Dog* (about an English springer spaniel) and *Gun Dog Breeds: A Guide to Spaniels, Retrievers, and Pointing Dogs*. He has also written a historical novel and a collection of essays on nature and country living.

"The Heart of My Hunting" first appeared in *A Breed Apart: A Tribute to the Hunting Dogs That Own Our Souls* (1993), a wonderful anthology edited by Doug Truax.

*Like this English springer, Charles Fergus's Jenny is a "rough-shooting" dog.* Photograph © Ron Spomer

IT NEVER SEEMED convenient. Hunting season was always just around the corner, and I didn't want her nursing puppies, or out of shape after having raised a litter, when the first day of grouse rolled around. I did not want a puppy for myself; I felt she should be my sole companion until she grew too old to put in a full day afield. So I kept putting it off, even though my hunting partners—after she'd made a particularly stirring flush or fetched a runner that surely would have fed the foxes—would scratch Jenny behind the ears, look at me, and ask, "When are you going to breed her?"

Jenny is an English springer spaniel. She is six years old, almost seven. Her coat is white, with patches of dark brown (technically, "liver") arrayed along her back and flanks, in what had looked to me, when she was a puppy, like the silhouette of a flushing grouse. Her tail is docked to about a foot in length, brown with an eye-catching white tip. Her eyes are golden-yellow. She has brown ears, a brown head, a white muzzle with a small brown mustache, and a symmetrical blaze on her forehead. Her shoulders reach to my knees. She is solid and muscular and, on the veterinarian's digital scale, weighs thirty-seven point six pounds.

Jenny is a rough-shooting dog. "Rough-shooting" is a British term that describes striking out across the land and taking whatever game the dog rousts out—precisely the sort of hunting Jenny and I practice here in central Pennsylvania.

To be sure, she is more than a hunting dog. She sounds the alarm when anyone drives down our lane. She can be counted on to join any sort of outing, be it a canoe trip, the one-hundred-yard walk to the mailbox, cross-country skiing (her first time out, she plunked down in the track to bite ice from between her pads, and suddenly we were both head-over-heels in the snow), my daily jog, picking blueberries (she strips them daintily from the stems with her front teeth and declines to drop them in the pail), hiking, bird watching, or simply puttering around in the yard. Jenny is a full-fledged member of our family, and confident in that status, but there is no question that she is my dog. Whenever the spirit moves her, which is often, she worms into my arms. She interposes herself between me and my four-year-old son when he and I are playing. Since she is not allowed on the furniture, she lays her head on my foot while I am sitting on the couch, reading. When I'm in my office writing, she curls up next to my chair.

Though she is not there now.

The house seems strangely empty. It has been like that all week. No friendly tail thumps when I lower a hand to pet her. No wagging and spinning at the door, as she lobbies to go outside. No gobs of white fur collecting in the corners, as my wife noted last weekend. However, I would bet that my wife, though she might not admit it, also misses Jenny.

On the bulletin board in my office is a list of five hunters who

*The Irish water spaniel is a first-class waterfowler bred for retrieving, unlike its flushing springer and cocker cousins.*
Photograph © Tara Darling

want a Jenny of their own. I would not have bred her just to satisfy these friends. But as Jenny matured—as she demonstrated the depth of her hunting instincts, her biddability and goodness of nature—I edged toward it. I did not make the decision lightly. I weighed and pondered and analyzed (and probably anthropomorphized) before I acted.

I remember how long it took me to pick a breed of dog in the first place. Before I got Jenny, I hunted with acquaintances who ran pointing dogs: Brittanys, English setters, and pointers. I enjoyed watching those dogs work. They were terrific at pointing woodcock, less adept at handling pheasants and grouse.

When a dog went on point, all too often I would spy the pheasant or grouse, its head down and its body hunched, legging it off through the brush. Or the dog would "bump" the bird, flush it prematurely. My friends warned me not to shoot at birds so bungled: It would encourage the dogs to run riot. On the days when everything clicked and we managed to shoot a bird over a point, rare was the dog who would then go and fetch it. A dog might point a dead bird, helping us locate it, but that technique failed when a wounded bird took off running. All of this puzzled me greatly. I had always thought that one of the reasons for hunting with a dog—perhaps the main reason—was that it would fetch the game.

I considered what was being asked of a pointing dog: upon encountering scent, to freeze, fight down the instinct to rush in and grab the prey; and then, after the shot, to abandon this static stance, perhaps chase down a runner, pick the bird up gently but firmly, and bring it back. From what I had read, some paragons consistently managed those contradictory tasks. But I felt I lacked the skill and patience to train a pointing dog to that level.

I wanted a more basic sort of canine, one that simply flushed the game, hustled it into the air with a sudden, dramatic rush. More important, I wanted a dog I could depend on to retrieve the game I downed. My dog would hunt the gamut of upland birds: grouse, woodcock, pheasants, doves. Since I planned to expand my hunting to include ducks, I needed a dog that also would dive into the swamp and recover what I shot. According to the books I read, the English springer spaniel could do all of those tasks, with aplomb and good cheer. And I was charmed by the breed's looks: trim, efficient, rough-and-ready, a touch feral-looking with those raggedy high-set ears.

It was a cool day in August, a day that spoke of autumn, when I went to pick up Jenny. The breeder let the mother and the puppies— three of the litter were left—out onto the lawn. I knelt and clapped my hands, and this double-handful of enthusiasm came tail wagging, ears flapping, as fast as her legs could carry her. I found it remarkable that a dog would so trust a strange human; but such is the nature of a puppy, open to love and to being loved. I have read about how early experiences imprint a creature and affect its behavior for the rest of its life. I became imprinted on Jenny at that moment, on that day in August of 1986.

Facing page: *A fly fisherman enjoys a day afield with a springer sidekick.* Photograph © Ron Spomer

*English springers along a summertime lakeshore*. Photograph © Sharon Eide/Elizabeth Flynn

I was thinking of that auspicious meeting—of the trust that Jenny had invested in me, and how it had grown and deepened—when I took her to the vet two weeks ago. I still had not decided whether to breed her, but I knew her time was limited. A six- or a seven-year-old bitch is far more likely to have problems whelping a litter than a three- or a four-year-old. If I was to breed Jenny at all, it would have to be during her next estrous.

What the veterinarian said added to my ambivalence. After examining her, he told me that Jenny had a constriction in her vagina. Some dogs, he said with a shrug, are just built that way. She might be able to accept a male, and she might not—in which case she could be bred through artificial insemination. That raised new questions in my mind. Once impregnated, would she be able to whelp? Probably, the vet said; and if need be, they could do a Caesarean section, a safe and routine procedure, some risk from the anesthesia, but usually without complications.

When Jenny and I got home that day, I grabbed my whistle and a pair of retrieving bucks. Down to the meadow we went, Jenny wagging her whole body and leaping for the dummies. This is old hat, but she loves it, loves to work, to do her job. I hupped her with a single blast on the whistle, threw a buck to one side, and heaved the second in the opposite direction. With a hand signal I sent her for the first buck; she raced to it and brought it back. I hupped her. "*Jenny!*" I said, releasing her for the second. She fetched it. I took the bucks, laid them down, and sat in the warm sun. Jenny sniffed the dummies, picked up one, and came and sat next to me.

When she was a puppy, she would carry all sorts of things in her mouth: sticks, pine cones, crumpled envelopes, corncobs filched from the compost heap, desiccated toads, songbirds that had broken their necks against the windows. Just holding something between her jaws seemed to make her feel secure. And how she loved to chase after the puppy buck—a small, kapok-filled boat bumper. She would pick it up with a flourish; her eyes knowing and her tail proud, she would dance it back to my hand.

One day—during her first October, when she was still too young to hunt—I shot a woodcock, carried it home, and hid it in the meadow. "*Jenny!*" I called, and waved her toward the bird. All gangly limbs and big paws, she romped along until she hit a tendril of scent— an essence she had never before encountered. She slammed to a halt, her body tense, her tail whipping from side to side. Guided by her nose, she sprang straight at the scent. Finding the source of that irresistible essence, she picked up the woodcock. I blew a few pips on the whistle. Fetching back, all the way she tried to stare at the strange feathery bundle between her jaws; it proved so enticing that she ran smack into my knee.

We spent hours in the meadow with whistle, buck, and gun. The guiding concept I drilled into her was *hup*. "Hup" is the traditional spaniel command for "sit." "Hup!" rockets out with authority to a dog on the edge of shotgun range, where "Sit!" may not be heard—or at least can be conveniently ignored. With that cornerstone firmly established, I could stop my spaniel on the trail of a running bird, so that I might get into position for a shot. Set her down when she got too near a road. Hide her at my side when ducks were flying. Halt her on a retrieve, then signal her to the bird.

I accustomed her to gunshots, to swimming, to riding in the canoe. Using planted birds (pigeons made dizzy and then hurled surreptitiously into the weeds), I tried to persuade her that the game always lay within twenty yards of the master's boots. Many were the Saturdays spent at a nearby shooting preserve run by a professional spaniel trainer; many were the pigeons, and finally the pheasants, that Jenny flushed and fetched. As we approached her second autumn, she had emerged as a spirited, hard-driving, raw, and promising young hunter.

One brisk October morning, we drove upstate in the dark, Jenny and I, and a friend and his young, equally inexperienced Labrador retriever. Dawn found us on the meandering headwaters of a stream, sneaking along, my friend and his dog on one bank, Jenny and I on the other. We crept past yellow-orange maples and deep green pines, through broad openings carpeted with tan grass and wine-red huckleberry. Frost lay heavily on the ground, and wisps of fog floated above the water.

Out ahead, we spotted a flock of wood ducks on a beaver pond. My friend and I crouched and began edging forward. Whispering fiercely, we held the dogs at heel. Soon our sneaking developed into a

Facing page: *A liver-and-white English springer spaniel in an autumn gamefield*. Photograph © Ron Spomer
Overleaf: *An English springer spaniel practices retrieving*. Photograph © Ron Spomer

hunched-over race with the ducks' and the dogs' increasing aware-
ness—until the flock finally took to the air with a chorus of keening
cries. Our shotguns rang out. Two ducks fell.

My friend's duck was killed outright, but mine was only wounded.
The dogs splashed around in a state of gleeful confusion. My duck, a
wood duck hen, swam off into the brush. Coming in from the side, I
spotted it only five yards ahead. Not wanting to obliterate it, I aimed a
few inches in front of its bill. I pulled the trigger, the water spouted—
and when it subsided, nothing was afloat. We searched for an hour. We
combed the alders lining the banks. The dogs stuck their noses in every
clump of brush, every patch of sedge. We looked upstream and down.
Finally we gave up; we continued on with our hunt, but after a few
hundred yards, we retraced our steps for one last look.

Jenny sniffed through a strip of grass we had searched maybe half a
dozen times. The fur across her shoulders stood up. She pounced. The
duck, peeping, went skidding down the bank in front of the spaniel
and splashed into the run. Jenny crashed in after it but came up empty.
I got her out and hupped her on the bank. After several minutes, my
friend noticed two small bumps emerging from the water beneath the
overhanging bank: the wood duck's eye and bill-tip. He shot. Jenny
made the five-yard fetch.

I drove down the valley. The windshield wipers snickered. The
creek, its surface dimpled with rain, ran brown and full on the south
side of the road. Jenny sat on the floor, on the passenger's side, her front
paws canted up onto the gearshift housing. She looked at me, then out
the rear window. The trees along the road whisked by, the gray hills
behind shifting more slowly. A crow flew across the road, and Jenny
spotted it, her eyes widening, her ears raising, her tail sweeping the
floorboards.

I had decided. This was her chance, her first and last chance, to pass
on that marvelous hunting sense, that loving merriness, that instinct
coming down through countless generations. That much she deserved.

The highway led past farms, houses, a lumberyard, a car dealership,
a gravel pit. Beyond the creek, the land sloped upward toward Brush
Mountain. Although it was late April, the mountain still looked like
November, the trees gray-brown and bare. In the valley the lawns were
greening, and weeping willows showed their tender yellow leaves. We
left the main road and drove along a winding street. My friend's house,
an old stone farmstead on three acres, is surrounded by newer homes.
The settlement lies on the fringe of a small city that has been slowly
crumbling for the last half-century, ever since its shops and yards—for
repairing rail cars and building locomotives—shut down.

My friend let out his springer, and we went down by the creek.
The male came after Jenny right away, sniffing at her tail, bumping her
with his shoulders. She kept spinning around to face him. When he got
too familiar, she growled him off.

The rain had slackened; my friend got a pigeon out of the bird
pen, dizzied it, and threw it into the pond. Jenny swims like an otter

(she has swum like that ever since she was a puppy—never that nervous forepaw-plunking that you see with some youngsters). With the male hupped on the bank, she paddled out, grabbed the pigeon, pirouetted in the water, and started back. Her white legs churned. Her eyes switched this way and that. She snorted water drops out of her nostrils. Her ears streamed back. Only the top of her head stayed dry.

We gave the male a retrieve. Then we let the dogs run. The male raced along close to Jenny, his side nudging hers. He licked Jenny's muzzle. He dropped to his belly, his rear end high and his tail wagging. She disdained to play with him. She came up to me, panting and wagging, a puzzled look on her face.

My friend's male, named Sky, is a young dog really coming into his own. Earlier this month, he placed third in a national pheasant competition held in Minnesota. Four years ago, my friend had gone to the Isle of Anglesey, off the coast of Wales, and bought the dog at the kennels of Talbot Radcliffe, the foremost springer spaniel breeder in the world. Sky's impeccable bloodline and his hunting prowess were not the only reasons I chose him: He is an experienced stud whom I hoped could effect the mating.

No luck that evening, though. Jenny would not stand for him; apparently she was not yet fully into estrous. It was dark when I said good-bye to her, there in the kennel by the creek. She barked plaintively as I crossed the lawn. I got in the truck and started for home. The traffic was light, and the rain had stopped.

The lights from a convenience store reflected off the black waters of the creek. Beyond loomed the mountain, dark and massive, probably with some good game cover tucked into its wooded folds. The combination of waters and woods got me thinking of another first from Jenny's first hunting season.

In the morning, I had shot two drake woodies on a beaver pond,

*Though originally bred as a woodcock hunter, the hunting cocker spaniel, particularly American cocker spaniels such as this one, were victims of their own popularity: Much of their hunting instinct was bred out of their nature by the numerous puppy mills operating to meet demand for the breed.* Photograph © Daniel Dempster

with Jenny retrieving both; back home, I exchanged hip boots for Bean boots, and we went to the bottoms along the creek, where the land starts its gradual slope to the mountain. We tried a big patch of hawthorn and crab apples that always holds grouse. Halfway into the cover, she showed scent. The grouse powered up and cartwheeled at my shot. I went to my knees and spotted it crumpled on the ground beneath the crabs' arching stems. The grouse shot up its head. Its glittering eye took in the onrushing dog, and the bird picked itself up and raced off through the leaves. Jenny matched it swerve for swerve. It scuttled down over the bank toward the creek. So great was my confidence that I sat, unloaded the gun, and waited for Jenny to return. She did, with the grouse in her mouth, its eye angry and its crest upraised. My heart was pounding as I took it from her. This passing of game between dog and man is the heart of my hunting. I looked at my rough-shooting dog, and she at me.

*An English springer nuzzles her pup.* Photograph © Alan and Sandy Carey

I swung the truck south at the light, gearing down for the hill. How far she had come since that first year! She had fetched many grouse—and would have fetched plenty more had I shot better. I would rather hunt

grouse than any other game. One day last season, I wounded a big male and Jenny chased him down and brought him in. The grouse had his head up. He looked positively ferocious, outraged at having been apprehended. He did something decidedly ungrouselike: Turned his face toward Jenny's and pecked at her eye. I took the bird and dispatched him, then checked Jenny. She must have blinked before he got her, for her eye was unhurt. Then, on the last day of the season—just three months back, up a little hollow not two miles from where I was now driving—I flushed twenty-seven grouse in a bit under four hours, did not kill a one, and did not begrudge the birds a thing. They were wild as hawks (Did they know it was the last day?), and Jenny couldn't handle them. The last bird was an exception: She caught him hiding in a blowdown, and drove him up, straight at me. A big bird with a broad chestnut tail. I turned to take him going away. He juked behind a bushy hemlock, and I never saw him again.

I stopped at another traffic light. The light changed, and I went east. Down the valley I drove. A good brushy valley where lights are few. I passed a shuttered-up country store, an auto body shop, an old barn with a hole battered in its brick side. Across the railroad tracks from the barn, on the other side of the stream, lies the covert I call Pufferbelly.

I named the covert that day, back in Jenny's first year, when an antique steam engine came chugging incongruously down the line. A gray day, with a chill wind to hurry the clouds. Quick showers of rain pattered against the fallen yellow leaves. The smoke from the locomotive hung like a banner above the tracks, then began shredding. We started from the east, into the wind. Immediately Jenny set to work with an almost frantic busyness to her quartering. Her lithe white form coursed through the brush like a predatory fish hunting in the shallows. The clouds parted for a moment, light slanting in through the break, lending a coppery tone to the aspens' water-beaded bark. Chalk on the ground, and holes made by bills probing for worms. Things can develop quickly—and often unpredictably—when you follow a flushing dog. The scent practically yanked her around. The woodcock came up like a gusted leaf. Wings twittering, following its mud-flecked bill, it swerved a course through the close-set trunks. My shot downed it on the far side of the creek. Jenny swam across, ferreted the bird out of the dense willows, and paddled back, her first woodcock dangling loose-headed and long-beaked from her jaws.

When I got back home, I looked at Jenny's empty kennel box. I sat down to read for a while, and no spaniel came to lay her head on my foot. I put the book down.

Was I tempting fate? I still did not think I wanted a pup for myself. I certainly wasn't breeding her for the money any puppies would bring. A friend once remarked that he was breeding his purebred dogs to put his kids through college. Put the vet's kids through college, is more like it.

So why press the issue? The next bitch I get, I'll have her spayed right off so I won't have to make these decisions. Had I done right by Jenny? Puppies were a tremendous drain on a dog, especially an older one. There was probably still time to call it off, the dogs were kenneled together but it didn't look like Sky would make any progress tonight.

But I didn't call. Pass it on, girl, I thought. If you can. That prebreeding exam—finding the constriction in her vagina—still bothered me. Artificial insemination? No. If she couldn't breed on her own, we'd forget it.

I sat in the quiet house, considering how much it meant to me, having Jenny. I remembered what was probably the brightest day of our first year's hunting. It was so cold that morning that my hands were alternately numb and then wracked with pain. Jenny had dipped her belly in the creek, and icicles tinkled when she wagged.

The decoys bobbed in the olive-drab water. A mallard quacked from somewhere downstream. Suddenly, there they were! Black ducks! Four pairs of wings came pumping, cupping, fluttering down—but the ducks flared up and began to flee. I managed to shove the safety off. I swung on the first duck in line, yanked the trigger, missed, shot again, apparently missed—and heard a splash. A duck, from farther back in line, floated upside down in the creek. "Jenny!"—and out she went into the frigid flow. Swimming hard, she gathered him in and was swept downstream by the current. She fought her way over to the bank. I stumbled through the brush and mud to meet her.

That afternoon, on a snowy hillside strewn with logging slash, she flushed and fetched a brace of grouse. Our hunt finished, we trudged home along the logging path as slivers of pink and yellow glowed in

*Tough to shake off the water when you're still up to your haunches in $H_2O$, but this otherwise brilliant English springer still tries to get rid of the excess wet stuff.* Photograph © Ron Spomer

the gray western sky. I walked loose-limbed and weary, basking in the sense that I understood, really understood, what it meant to collaborate with a dog. To expand my instincts in partnership with a creature whose talents far surpassed mine. To let her joyousness, her simplicity, rub off on me. To shed mind and intellect for a time, to soak up the hunt, to simply be myself. I called her to me. As she danced around, her eyes on the cover, still wanting to get in there and hunt, I aimed caresses at her head. I ran my hand down her back and crooked it where her muscular hind leg joined her belly. I pulled her against my own leg, held her there for a moment, and told her what a good dog she was. With a perfunctory tail wag she broke free, and, glancing over her shoulder, tried to lure me back into the slash. I smiled and patted

*An English springer spaniel snoozes away, dreaming of grouse and autumn days afield.* Photograph © Tara Darling

my palm against my thigh;
reluctantly, she came back to
heel. She had no need to stop
and ponder, no need to hoard
memories. For her, there was
only the sweet now.

Another evening, in the truck
again; the moon was setting in
the west behind coal-sack clouds
as I headed for home. Tonight it
was done—though she will stay
with the male for a while yet.

She was ready. She was
flagging her tail, wanting it to
happen despite the discomfort
causing her to yelp and pull away.
I ended up holding Jenny, talking
quietly to her, and there was
blood and pain, and then calm,
and, for the humans at least,
elation. Who knows what the
dogs thought and felt?

There will be more blood
and pain nine weeks hence. I
hope someday to write a postscript about healthy young
spaniels on their way to good
homes, to lives that are rich with
love of master and land and game
and the consuming, fulfilling
passion of the hunt. I hope to
write a postscript about an old
rough-shooting dog back home
in the fields and marshes, the
beaver dams, the thornapple
patches, the alder tangles, having
passed on her brief, glowing
spark.

# PART IV

# The Spirit of the Spaniel

*"I wish men could accept life as spaniels do."*
—Blanche Shoemaker Wagstaff, *Bob, The Spaniel,* 1927

Above: *An Irish water spaniel enjoys a stroll with its owner.* Photograph ©
Kent and Donna Dannen
Left: *The English cocker spaniel: intelligent, friendly, and just plain good
looking.* Photograph © Kent and Donna Dannen

# The Lord of Life

## by E.V. Lucas

 "The spaniel tribes are gentle, docile, easily attached to man . . ." Harriet Beecher Stowe wrote in *Our Dogs and Other Stories* (1862). Indeed, spaniels are a happy bunch of hounds, a menagerie of distinctly beautiful dogs tied together by kindness and devotion. The merriness and decency of spaniels is infectious; with a spaniel in the house you can't help but don rose-colored glasses.

Edward Verrall Lucas lucidly portrays this "spaniel spirit" in "The Lord of Life." A prolific essayist, critic, and travel writer, Lucas authored some 137 books—and edited several more—during a long career in journalism and publishing. Though he wrote about dogs at times during his career, he was primarily known as a travel writer, essayist, and biographer. He penned dozens of travel books, authored numerous essays for the British magazine *Punch*, and wrote what is still considered the standard biography of Charles Lamb, the British critic, essayist, and author. In fact, it was not until 1927, a full thirty-five years after his career began, that Lucas compiled his dog stories in the book *The More I See of Men: Stray Essays on Dogs*, from which the tale "The Lord of Life" is taken. After reading the story, you will wonder what took him so long to turn his attention to things canine.

*The affectionate and gentle English cocker spaniel has much in common with its American cousin.*
Photograph © Robert and Eunice Pearcy

IN HIS PRESCRIPTION for the perfect home Southey included a little girl rising six years and a kitten rising six weeks. That is perhaps the prettiest thing that ever found its way from his pen—that patient, plodding, bread-winning pen, which he drove with such pathetic industry as long as he had any power left with which to urge it forward. A little girl rising six years and a kitten rising six weeks. Charming, isn't it?

But, my dear rascally Lake Poet, what about a puppy rising six months? How did you come to forget that?—such a puppy as is in this room as I write: a small black puppy of the Cocker spaniel blood, so black that had the good God not given him a gleaming white corner to his wicked little eye, one would not know at dinner whether he was sitting by one's side or not—not, that is, until his piercing shrieks, signifying that he had been (very properly) trodden on again, rent the welkin.

This puppy have I called the Lord of Life because I cannot conceive of a more complete embodiment of vitality, curiosity, success, and tyranny. Vitality first and foremost. It is incredible that so much pulsating quicksilver, so much energy and purpose, should be packed into a foot and a half of black hide. He is up earliest in the morning, he retires last at night. He sleeps in the day, it is true, but it is sleep that hangs by a thread. Let there be a footfall out of place, let a strange dog in the street venture but to breathe a little louder than usual, let the least rattle of plates strike upon his ear, and his sleep is shaken from him in an instant. From an older dog one expects some of this watchfulness. But when an absurd creature of four months with one foot still in the cradle is so charged with vigilance, it is ridiculous.

If nothing occurs to interest him, and his eyes are no longer heavy (heavy! he never had heavy eyes), he will make drama for himself. He will lay a slipper at your feet and bark for it to be thrown. I admire him most when he is returning with it in his mouth. The burden gives him responsibility: his four black feet, much too big for his body, all move at once with a new importance and rhythm. When he runs for the slipper he is just so much galvanized puppy rioting with life; when he returns he is an official, a guardian, a trustee; his eye is grave and responsible; the conscientious field spaniel wakes in him and asserts itself.

As to his curiosity, it knows no bounds. He must be acquainted with all that happens. What kind of a view of human life a dog, even a big dog, acquires, I have sometimes tried to imagine by kneeling or lying full length on the ground and looking up. The world then becomes strangely incomplete: one sees little but legs. Of course the human eye is set differently in the head, and a dog can visualize humanity without injuring his neck as I must do in that grovelling posture; but none the less the dog's view of his master standing over him must be very partial, very fragmentary. Yet this little puppy, although his eyes are within eight inches of the ground, gives the

Facing page: *An English springer spaniel gets a hug.* Photograph © Isabelle Francais

*A stylish American cocker sports a polka-dotted headband.* Photograph © Kent and Donna Dannen

impression that he sees all. He goes through the house with a microscope.

But for his dependence, his curiosity, and his proprietary instinct to be studied at their best, you should see him in an empty house. All dogs like to explore empty houses with their masters, but none more than he. His paws never so resound as when they patter over the bare boards of an empty house. He enters each room with the eye of an auctioneer, a builder, tenant, furnisher and decorator in one. I never saw such comprehensive glances, such a nose for a colour scheme. But leave him by accident behind a closed door and see what happens. Not the mandrake torn bleeding from its earth ever shrieked more melancholy. Yet tears are instant with him always, in spite of his native cheerfulness. It was surely a puppy that inspired the proverb about crying before you are hurt.

I spoke of his success. That is perhaps his most signal characteristic, for the world is at his feet. Whether indoors or out, he has his own way, instantly follows his own inclination. It is one of his most charming traits that he thinks visibly. I often watch him thinking. "Surely it's time tea was brought," I can positively see him saying to himself. "I hope that cake wasn't finished yesterday: it was rather more decent than usual. I believe those girls eat it in the kitchen." Or, "He's putting on his heavy boots: that means the hill. Good! I'll get near the door so as to be sure of slipping out with him." Or, "It's no good: he's not going for a walk this morning. That stupid old desk again, I suppose." Or, "Who was that? Oh, only the

postman. I shan't bark for him." Or, "I'm getting awfully hungry. I'll go and worry the cook."

But the most visible token of his success is the attention, the homage, he receives from strangers. For he not only dominates the house, but has a procession of admirers after him in the streets. Little girls and middle-aged ladies equally ask permission to pat him. Old gentlemen ask if he is for sale, and inquire his price. Not that he looks valuable—as a matter of fact, though pure he is not remarkable—but that he suggests so much companionship and fun. One recognizes instantly the Vital Spark.

When it comes to the consideration of his tyranny, there enters a heavy spaniel named Bush and a dainty capricious egoist in blue-grey whom we will call Smoke. Smoke once had a short way with dogs; but the Lord of Life has changed all that. Smoke once would draw back a paw of velvet, dart it forward like the tongue of a serpent and return to sleep again, perfectly secure in her mind that that particular dog would harass her no more. But do you think she ever hurt the puppy in that way? Never. He loafs into the room with his hands in his pockets and his head full of mischief, perceives a long bushy blue-grey tail hanging over the edge of the sofa, and forthwith gives it such a pull with his teeth as a Siberian householder who had been out late and had lost his latch-key might at his door-bell when the wolves were after him. An ordinary dog would be blinded for less; but not so our friend. Smoke merely squeaks reproach, and in a minute or two, when the puppy has tired a little of the game, he is found not only lying beside her and stealing her warmth, but lying in the very centre of the nest in the cushion that she had fashioned for herself. Tyranny, if you like!

And Bush? Poor Bush. For every spoiled new-comer there is, I suppose, throughout life an old, faithful friend who finds himself on the shelf. It is not quite so bad as this with Bush, and when the puppy grows up and is staid too, Bush will return to his own again; but I must admit that at the beginning he had a very hard time of it. For the puppy, chiefly by hanging on his ear, first infuriated him into sulks, and then, his mastery being recognized, set to work systematically to tease and bully him. The result is that now Bush actually has to ask permission before he dares to take up his old seat by my chair; he may have it only if the puppy does not want it.

But Bush is not my theme; Bush was never a Lord of Life: his pulse was always a little slow, his nature a little too much inclined to accept rather than initiate. Nor, I suppose, will our Lord of Life be quite such a Lord much longer, for with age will come an increase of sobriety, a diminution of joy. That he will not untimely fall by the way, but will grow up to serious spanielhood, I feel as sure as if an angel had fore-warned me; but were he now to die this should be his epitaph: "Here lies a Lord of Life, aged six months. He would never be broken to the house, but after sin was adorable."

*The intelligence of the Irish water spaniel emanates from this beautiful dog.* Photograph © Judith E. Strom

# Ruffled Paws

## *by* Bertha Damon

 *A Sense of Humus*, Bertha Damon's elegant 1943 book, is a largely autobiographical tale of life in rural New England. Blending fact and fiction in essays on gardening and nature with further reflections on life in the country, Damon weaves a story so many of us would like to tell about ourselves: the story of her passions and her life.

Damon authored two other books during her lifetime, the best-selling *Grandma Calls It Carnal* (1938) and *Green Corners* (1947). In addition to her writing, Damon earned her livelihood building and remodeling houses. She divided her time between a home in New Hampshire and a home in California, living her life as she liked and occasionally putting her experiences down on paper.

"Ruffled Paws," the story of the little cocker pup that wins over the hearts of both Damon and her husband, originally appeared in *A Sense of Humus*.

Does a dog which marries into a family along with his mistress ever fit into the new picture easily and immediately, I wonder. Dogs suffer jealousy; the passion is not unknown in man. Are a husband, a wife, and such a dog what is meant by the eternal triangle?

One might summon Elizabeth Barrett's cocker spaniel Flush from the spirit world and ask him. Or summon Elizabeth herself. She ought to know; she understood cockers. With her large-eyed sensitive face, framed in long curls, she even looked like one. (She herself recognized the likeness, and with pleasure.) It is biography that Flush bit the suitor who was Robert Browning. It is history that Josephine's dog, backed up by Josephine, insisted on sleeping with Napoleon in the imperial bed, greatly to Napoleon's annoyance. It is even rumored that the mighty conqueror was bitten by the dog in the argument.

It seems there are two schools of thought holding sharply conflicting theories as to just where dogs should sleep. I myself before I ever had a dog would have repudiated the idea that I would permit one to sleep on my bed, let alone want one to. And the day I brought home a small cocker puppy—still I had no intention of such an arrangement; it was the puppy's own idea, strongly held to. It has turned out through many years to be a good one. Wherever Mickey and I found ourselves, alone in some spooky house I was rebuilding, or in a strange hotel, or in a camping site in the wild Sierra, I had only to pat a place near my feet and say, "Come, lie down, Mickey. It's our home." And it was that for both of us.

From Stella Benson, who, as Christopher Morley observed, saw with extraordinary intuition the feelings and gestures of animals—and even of buildings and automobiles—I learned much of what goes on in the minds of dogs and in the minds of dog lovers as well. She used to say that the real dog lover is invariably someone who has been hurt by life and needs a better opinion of himself, and that there is something in the quality of a dog's admiration that gives this to him. From experience I have learned the strange truth that a dog's faithful presence through the night and his approval of me in the morning do have the power to remove a feeling of inadequacy and to replace it with courage and a little inner grin; that the indifference of the vast universe and the insignificance of the self make a quite satisfactory union if the catalytic agent is a dog who loves you. Nevertheless, some there are who disapprove of dogs in bedrooms.

And in dining rooms, when it comes to that. Mickey in pre-New Hampshire days had been accustomed to be in the dining room with the other people. He didn't get in the way; for his own peace of mind he always stayed in the safety zone inside the stretchers of the serving table. A cat claws and miaows when you eat, draws itself up to be a thorny vine twining round you, but a dog who has not been spoiled lies down at some distance and looks tactfully away, pretending you are not eating lest you be embarrassed by a sense of your selfishness. It was not the food that attracted Mickey, but the sociability. If man can be

*An American cocker spaniel trio.* Photograph © Robert and Eunice Pearcy

classified as a social animal, so can dogs. Mickey, even when asleep or seeming so, would dreamily thump his tail when happy laughter burst out. But notwithstanding these extenuating circumstances, his presence in the dining room was known to be unwelcome.

Also there was here a novel standard of instant obedience. Any cocker when summoned is likely to run gaily in the opposite direction with a merry backward glance, not that he is disobedient but that he thinks it will be fun to do something different from what he is told. When cockers are puppies they are so tenderhearted that if you speak to one not sternly but just seriously, he turns over on his back, prayerfully folds his ruffled paws out of harm's way, and says, "Here am I. Whip me if you must, if the strange madness has come upon you to whip your faithful dog, whose only fault is in loving you too well." This has the effect of relaxing discipline. Such fundamentals of cocker psychology I understood; there were an influential few who did not.

I thought and thought, and at last I conceived a bold plan. ("Grandma," I had said abruptly in one of those days when I was poring over the Adam-and-Eve-in-the-Garden story, "Grandma, what does conceive mean?"

("It—what are you reading there, Bertha? Oh. Well, conceive means—means imagine."

("That doesn't make sense," I said, small forefinger on the text. "It says here, 'And Adam knew Eve his wife and she conceived and bare Cain.'"

("Yes, it does make sense," said Grandma. "Adam knew Eve, that is, got acquainted with her and after that she conceived, that is, imagined, she was going to have a baby. And she did. His name was Cain. You go out to the woodpile right away and bring in some wood.")

Now, I imagined that if I got my husband a puppy, a very young cocker puppy, for him to bring up, it would take his eye off my dog; and I felt quite sure that no matter what he did with his cocker its resultant behavior would not be so flawless that he could say anything about flaws in my dog's behavior—not consistently. And I knew my husband to be a pearl of consistency. I thought the chosen puppy had better be a female, all tenderness and worship.

By what seemed a remarkable coincidence, my next trip to Boston took me by a kennel of cockers. I stopped, and selected a small three-month-old bundle of curls and love and timidity. I brought her home in my car—not without several contretemps—and in due season laid her gently in my husband's lap.

"A present for your birthday next week," I said, looking harmless as doves, "a present from me." (Was that a shadow on his face?) "But you needn't keep her," I added quickly, "if she doesn't appeal to you. I haven't paid for her. She is on approval and can be returned within ten days."

Politely he touched her with a thumb almost as big as one of her folded paws.

"It was good of you to think of it," he said, "but really this isn't the breed I prefer. We'll just take care of it until you can return it conveniently."

By and by I brought a little dish of chopped meat and a cup of warm milk, with the suggestion that he himself and none other should administer them. I left him alone with his puppy-on-approval. She had silky ears. All day I kept away at each feeding time; the kind man fed her and she was grateful to him. She began to follow him a little. She had long eyelashes. The first night he arranged for her, back of the kitchen stove, a warm nest of his second-best flannel trousers, and that first night there she slept—or, rather, there she wept. The next day she followed him more. She was auburn gold all over, except for the little cream-colored ruffles that hung down behind like a frilled petticoat. In fact, that second night she followed him to bed and she slept with him. I did not openly notice this development. The next day she followed him all the time.

At the end of a week I went into my husband's study where he sat at his desk jabbing away at a manuscript with a blue pencil, and the puppy sat adoring in the best upholstered chair, pulled near for her convenience.

*A Sussex spaniel behind the wheel.*
Photograph © Isabelle Francais

"Come on, puppy," I said, picking her up casually, "back you go to Massachusetts. Too bad! You're not the breed the Master likes."

"Put my dog down!" said my husband. "That's *my* dog. Her name is Betsey, and you leave her alone." So from then on she was his, his Betsey the Beloved, Betsey the—the Witch.

All went well.

Betsey the Beloved was never again asked to sleep in the kitchen; she slept regularly in her master's bedroom; she slept on his bed; more than that, she slept in his bed with him, under the bedclothes. On his bare feet she slept, in an utter abnegation of comfort, and almost of respiration, in an ultimate expression of love, of desire deeper than life for nearness to her Beloved. There—except on the hottest of nights in July or August—across his naked feet she always slept, except occasionally when she had to emerge as a whale does for air. Betsey the Beloved. Betsey the Witch.

"I notice Betsey doesn't sleep in the kitchen as dogs should," I just couldn't help saying to the master at last. "I notice she sleeps in bed with you."

"Well, yes, she does. I haven't changed my mind, I tell you. I still think that having a dog on one's bed is unsanitary, it's undisciplined, it's sentimental. I think"—he burst out—"I think it's disgraceful! But somehow—that's where she sleeps. I can't seem to keep her from doing so."

"Don't you like it that way?"

"Well—yes—er—in a way I do. But have you never heard," he added with a self-deprecating grin, "that the worst thing ever said about slavery was that the slave liked it?"

*A lovable "bundle of curls," the cocker spaniel will quickly capture your heart.* Photograph © Judith E. Strom

Usually our New Hampshire nights are cool. But on one of those hot still nights that sometimes lie oppressive, just as I had managed to fall into a restless sleep, I was wakened by my husband's voice from the adjoining room.

"It *is* hot, isn't it, you poor dear?" he said.

I was sleepily rallying myself to make proper meteorological reply, but unencouraged he went right on.

"How you pant, darling," he said.

Goodness, had I been panting so loud as all that?

"Shall I get up and get you some water, sweetheart . . ."

Maybe this was the hottest night that ever was and I had not realized it. Just as I was catching my breath to call out, "Yes, thanks ever so much," he concluded—

"Water, poor little Betsey?"

Huh!

The rule against dogs in dining rooms was blessedly lost sight of. Betsey was in the dining room every mealtime, often close to her master's feet and often out in the runway, obliging the hired girl to walk around on the wrong side. She would sit up and put out the most feminine of paws with dainty ruffled wrist and touch a guest ever so gently, reminding him courteously that his enjoyment of his

Above: *A great big smooch from an English springer spaniel pup.* Photograph © Marilyn "Angel" Wynn
Overleaf: *An English springer spaniel on the California coast.* Photograph © Sharon Eide/Elizabeth Flynn

victual was greedy, that he was negligent of the needs of a languishing lady cocker. The most selfish gourmet could not enjoy his food until he had fed Betsey. Her master fed her too, the best bits on his plate if I was not looking. And I never was.

Very early Betsey went in for automobile chasing as her chief sport, and the day came when her master told her clearly—in so many words—that if she chased another car he would thrash her, thrash her in sight of all the world. She listened docilely, and so the very next time a car came down our grassy driveway she gave one glad yelp and dashed after it and around it in circles and straight at it—to make it stop. From the corner of her eye she saw her master rise with dignity from his seat among his guests on the porch. Down across the deep lawn and back again and around the house she encouraged him to chase her and then, precisely in front of all the audience on the porch, she permitted him to overtake her. Somewhere along the route he had grabbed a lily stalk, and now he raised it high. Betsey neatly laid herself on her back at his feet, her ruffled paws uplifted, gazed tenderly at him through her long eyelashes, and said, "Strike me, oh beloved—if you can."

Even Betsey's back-seat driving was pleasing to her master— Betsey's was. She was a back-seat driver of the most apprehensive sort. She would look far ahead to spy out a mud hole or a rough spot in the road and begin to yelp, "Yip, yip! How in the world are we ever going to get around that? Careful, now! Yip, ow, wow! Oh, do take care! Ow, yip, yip, wow!" However long the trip, she never allowed herself one moment's relaxation in sleep. Occasionally she permitted herself the pleasure of leaning out to envy birds or butterflies or to put some large he-dog in his place, but most of the time she looked as if she were clinging desperately to the mast.

It was well for all of us that Betsey was a part of our little world, and for Mickey not least. She brought out all that was chivalrous in him. Someone has said that a dog is the only animal who consistently shows consideration for his female. Be that as it may, Mickey again and again gave up to Betsey his own highly prized dinner—in the dish that said DOG on it—never trying to drive her away, even though she drove him away most petulantly. Sometimes the sight of Betsey the Beloved turning from her own dinner, which nevertheless she gave him to understand was by no means discarded, and gobbling his with rude bitchy growls, was almost too much for him to bear and he would come and find me and protest in plaintive tones of self-pity. But to the proud beauty herself he said never a word.

For Betsey's sake he broke a strict rule he had made, never to bite a porcupine again, never. A porcupine, sure of himself as he is, is the only animal which cordially offers to let an inexperienced dog bite his behind. Mickey had accepted the first offer, he had accepted the second, and each time he had come away with a torturing beard and mouthful of barbed quills. Thereafter his policy was *laissez faire, laissez aller*. But Betsey, out of sheer wantonness, loved to meet a porcupine

Facing page: *An English cocker spaniel retrieves the mail*. Photograph © Tara Darling

*What's cuter than a Cavalier King Charles spaniel? A Cavalier King Charles spaniel puppy, of course.* Photograph ©
Sharon Eide/Elizabeth Flynn

somewhere in the woods, to lead the villain on, and then to flee, calling in hysterical maidenly barks for Mickey her hero to save her from a fate worse than death.

How sweet are looks that ladies bend on whom their favors fall; for them I battle to the end to save from shame and thrall—and so Mickey, forgetting the torturing quills, the bloody pliers jerking them out, or perhaps not forgetting but daring all again for Betsey's sake, would pitch into the spiky porcupine and wrestle with him, while Betsey removed her beautiful self to a near-by place of safety from which she might watch the gratifying carnage.

Samule always refers to a certain class of carefree bitches as "spaded," which sounds pretty darn thorough. Contrary to Uncle John's advice, we never had Betsey spaded, and so it came about that the best summer ever was that one when Mickey and Betsey were blessed with a family of five. At the beginning of our first call to inquire after Betsey and her babies, she was apologetic.

"Oh, dear, look at all this," she said deprecatingly, crawling forward and laying her head on her master's beloved foot, "look at all this. But I really couldn't help it."

We praised her until she was convinced that she had achieved something that surely no other bitch had ever been clever enough to achieve before, and her maternal pride bordered on arrogance.

Honesty compels me to admit that Betsey was never a model mother. Her one thought was for her master. While the puppies in their nursery in the barn would be wailing and yiping for warmth and maternal counsel and above all for supper, she would come sauntering along from somewhere and hop up lightly on her master's bed, intending to spend the night there. Over and over again I would have to chase Betsey, catch her, carry her to the puppies, and feed her to them by main force.

As soon as the little ones were big enough to leave the nursery, auburn waves rippled after me wherever I went, but I thought it best in general to encourage the puppies to spend more time outdoors than in. One discovers, while bringing up a litter of puppies, the long-sought fountain of youth which, like many other things, has had its value increased by legendary rumor and is not precisely what had been hoped for.

Betsey herself had always had a charming way of hunting butterflies which were, of course, where butterflies should be—hovering over the best blossoms. She would take off from anywhere on the porch or the lawn and come down smash! among the bright fragile poppies. She taught this to her puppies, all of them at once, and it was a pretty sight to see. Their golden tail tips wagging among the plants looked like butterflies of a livelier sort. Well, yes, the puppies dug holes sometimes, and sometimes they rolled down a few plants. But what of it? When hail beats the garden flat, we accept it as an act of God. Well, puppies are an act of God, and one of his very pleasantest. I believe in a balanced universe: some poppies and some puppies. To miss the joy is to miss all.

In fact, I didn't mind when Uncle John's teeth were ravished. Of late he has become quite careless about his uppers and unders—isn't that the last infirmity of noble mind, and not what Milton said?—and one day Uncle John was making a great to-do because he wanted to dress for golf and couldn't lay hands on his teeth anywhere. He swore he had left them rolled in his handkerchief on a corner of the porch magazine rack. The entire household was pressed into the search, which spread all over the porch and into the house, upstairs and down. We had just come from dismantling the east bathroom and were all assembled on the porch explaining to Uncle John he couldn't have left his teeth on the magazine rack or they would be there now, teeth certainly don't walk off by themselves, when out of the corner of my eye I saw down near the apple tree an unusually gay and active knot of puppies. There was something suspicious in their excited competition for some obviously rare treasure.

I have learned never to leave a family group abruptly enough to cause inquiry, but just to melt out of it. I melted and was presently down where the puppies were tussling and garglingly growling and giggling. One of them turned toward me with a wide grin, being temporarily possessed of Uncle John's uppers. Two other puppies were disputing the honor of the unders. I detached these features of Uncle John's from the regretful infants, wiped them off, not as thoroughly as I could have wished, and, the family by now being off on another tack in quest of hidden treasure, I sneaked them into the magazine rack.

A little later Uncle John salvaged them, pointing out that he had been right all the time, he *had* left them in the magazine rack. There they were all the time—his teeth, unquestionably his. He did not notice that the puppies had made some indentures.

All in all, it was Betsey the Witch who through our ever-circling years brought in an age of gold, when Discipline never raised its ugly head and everywhere was peace and good will to dogs. Once in a while, to be sure, Uncle John would look thoughtfully at Betsey snuggling hour after hour on her master's left arm while he with his right worked away as best he could at a manuscript—Uncle John would look at Betsey snuggling there, never turning her head, only rolling her brown amber eyes at any who might pass; and Uncle John would say that she ought to be pampered less in general and above all ought to be trained to obedience when outdoors. He explained how the latter could be done.

"What you ought to do, Lindsay, is to get a spike collar and put on her, and a long stout chain. Take her out walking. Call her to heel, and when she doesn't obey—and that young bitch is sure not to—you just jerk the chain sharply till the spikes jab her neck. She'll learn after a few experiences of that."

"No doubt," my husband would reply, gently stroking Betsey's velvet drooping ears, and quite forgetful that he himself had once suggested that very discipline for another person and another cocker to follow. "No doubt. By the way, Uncle John, don't you think this looks like a good day for golf?"

(Ah, sweet little Betsey of the dainty ruffled paws, the fringed bright eye, and coquettish glance—where are you now? Sometimes in the night it rains and I wake from a dream and know you are not in our house and I think, "Oh, we have forgotten Betsey and left her out-doors in the night." Then, waking, I remember that in more Elysian fields than ours you chase bright butterflies.)

*A pair of well-groomed American cocker spaniels behind a wrought-iron fence.* Photograph © Kent and Donna Dannen

# Sandy's Golf Dog

## *by* Horace Lytle

J. Horace Lytle was a dog man. Born in Ohio, Lytle dabbled in a variety of occupations until 1919, when he established the J. Horace Lytle Company, an advertising firm in Dayton. But dogs and dog field trials were his avocation, and this interest, combined with his talent for the written word, led to his appointment as an editor for *Field & Stream* magazine in 1925. His specialty was hunting dogs, and for some twenty years Lytle wrote or co-wrote the magazine's column on gun dogs. He also found time to write several books, including *Bird Dog Days* (1926), *No Hunting?* (1928), *Gun Dogs Afield* (1942), and *Simple Secrets of Dog Discipline* (1946).

"Sandy's Golf Dog" is the tale of a talented Clumber spaniel that saves the day. It originally appeared in Lytle's 1920 book *The Story of Jack, a Tale of the North and Other Fascinating Dog Stories.*

*Like this Clumber spaniel, Horace Lytle's Bruce is always ready for a day on the links.* Photograph ©
Judith E. Strom

SANDY MCDONALD HAD been our professional at the Grossmere Country Club for two years. When he came to us he brought with him his dog Bruce, a Clumber Spaniel.

Bruce must have been more than ten or eleven years old even at that time; he was so old that he soon became almost blind. Once having established himself in his new quarters at the golf shop, he seldom left the place, and I don't recall ever having gone in for my clubs that he was not there, lying on his pillow behind the door.

He was too old to be good for anything, if in fact he ever had been, but it was evident from the care and attention Sandy bestowed on him that his master held for him a most unusual affection. "Watch out, gentlemen, be careful of Bruce there," had been the solicitous warning to many of us golfers as we had gone into the shop for our clubs or to interview Sandy.

One day when I went out with three other fellows to play in a foursome, Sandy was not there—nor was Bruce. And we did not learn the cause until after we had finished our match and adjourned to the proverbial "nineteenth hole" to hold the usual post mortem of a golf game.

"Where's Sandy to-day?" I asked of the boy who served us.

"His ol' dog died, sir, an' Sandy laid off. You should 'ave seen the way he carried on 'round here this morning. A fellow wouldn't think Sandy could feel so bad 'bout anythin' as he did 'bout that dog."

"I asked Sandy once what the dog was good for besides sleeping," said Jim Stone, "and I got such a crusty reply that I never mentioned the beast to him again in any manner, shape, or form."

"What else could you expect in the circumstances?" I asked. "No man likes to have fun made of his dog. I never tried, but I believe, if asked in the right way, that Sandy would be glad to tell about Bruce. In fact, I'm going to try it—for Sandy's love for that dog was so far above the ordinary that I've an idea there must be some special reason for it."

"I wish you luck," Jim said. "I'm sure I wouldn't mention the cur to him again for a hundred dollars."

"Well, I'll tell you all about it some time, after I've seen Sandy," was my only reply as I sipped my lemonade.

"A box of balls you don't get any satisfaction," Jim remarked with a smile.

"Taken," I answered, "and you other fellows to be the judges."

"Agreed," said Jim. "We'll settle it right here next Saturday—I believe we're going to play the same foursome."

Before my wager with Jim, I had never had more than a mild curiosity regarding Sandy's dog; now, however, it was different—in fact, I became so possessed with the desire that on Wednesday I telephoned Sandy and made an engagement with him for Thursday morning. An odd time for a business man to be taking a golf lesson, but I figured we might eat lunch together at the club, which would be a fine chance for me to

*Facing page: A Welsh springer spaniel pup retrieves a mouth-stretching tennis ball. Photograph © Judith E. Strom*

*The Clumber spaniel is the portliest of the spaniels but has an innate talent for locating everything from woodcock to golf balls.* Photograph © Isabelle Francais

hear all about Bruce.

I paved the way while we were in the golf shop just before lunch, by inquiring:

"So you lost poor old Bruce, didn't you? Awfully sorry to hear it. What kind of dog was he, Sandy?"

For a minute or so I doubted what his answer was going to be. I could see that he was regarding me very carefully to decide whether or not I was serious. I was—and Sandy so decided.

"I haven't ever said much about Bruce around here," he began, "for I knew most of the men didn't even know about him, and the way some of them felt I never cared to tell them."

"I'm fond of dogs, Sandy, and I'd truly like to hear the story of Bruce—if you care to tell me."

He looked at me thoughtfully again—then: "I believe you, Mr. Welty, and I'll tell it to you. He was a wonderful dog, sir."

"Fine, Sandy. Let's go in and get lunch, and you can tell me then."

"Good," he agreed—and this is the story he told me a few minutes later:

"Bruce was a full-blooded Clumber Spaniel, Mr. Welty, though he'd gotten so old and coarse that you might not have realized it. I got him in the old country when he was just a wee bit of a pup. He was extra well bred, his sire having been one of England's greatest champions. Bruce was given to me by a man who was always grateful that I taught him how to make a real mashie pitch to the hole. He was one of the hardest to teach I ever saw, but finally the knack of it just came to him, and after that his approach was about his best shot.

"When I first got Bruce he was that small I could put him in my pocket. He was the cutest mite of a pup you ever saw—and his favorite plaything was a golf ball. He was raised playing with golf balls, and he'd roll them around on the floor by the hour without getting tired of it. His favorite stunt was to bat the ball with his paw, or shove it with his nose, and then chase it.

"After he got bigger I taught him to go get a ball when I'd throw it and bring it back to me. He learned to do this so well, and liked it so well, that after a while I got so I'd drive old balls out into the rough with a golf club and send Bruce for them. He got so good at this that he mighty seldom ever lost a ball—in fact, I might say he never did."

"A pretty convenient sort of dog to have, I should say, Sandy."

"I guess you'll say so by the time you've heard more about him," was Sandy's reply. And then he continued:

"As Bruce got bigger I had a hard time to leave him behind when I went out to play, for we were such pals that he wanted to be with me all the time; but I did finally begin taking him instead of a caddie when giving lessons, and he would fetch the balls back for us.

"One day he got out of the shop and followed me when I was going out to play, but he insisted on chasing the balls and gave me so much trouble that I had to have the caddie lead him back to the shop

and lock him up.

"But another day soon after that I decided that, as I'd taught Bruce to fetch a golf ball back to me, I could also teach him to let them alone when I wanted him to. In attempting this I had to undo much that I'd already done, and it was hard work, with no indication, for a long time at least, that I would be successful. 'You can't teach an old dog new tricks,' and Bruce, although not an old dog by any means, was nevertheless pretty headstrong about changing from his earlier teachings and inclinations.

"I kept at him, however, more determined all the time to succeed with him. And I did! I might not have been able to do it with most dogs, but Bruce was smarter than any other dog I ever saw, and he was so fond of me that he was anxious to try to please me and do what I wanted of him. And once started, we made good progress.

"It took a lot of patience on my part, but I finally got him trained. When, as in practice or giving lessons, I wanted him to bring the ball back to me, I would say, 'Go fetch, Bruce—fetch ball.' And when I only wanted him to go to the ball without touching it, I'd say, 'Now stand, Bruce—find ball—stand.'

"After a while he got so he knew himself what times I wanted him to bring the ball, and when I merely wanted him to find it. His work and stand on point of a golf ball were worthy of the best pointer or setter that I ever saw on birds. I even trained him perfectly to 'heel' when not hunting a lost ball, and also, when in a match, never to follow me nearer the hole than the edge of the green. Thus he was never in the way, or the slightest possible bother to my opponents. He became absolutely perfect on a golf course. I tell you, Mr. Welty, there never was another dog like him."

"From what you've been telling me, Sandy, I believe you're right," and I was soon to have this opinion confirmed, for Sandy went right ahead with the story.

"As his work became more and more perfect, Bruce helped me to win many a match where a lost ball would have turned the tide against me—and he became known all over both England and Scotland.

"And then, one day before the championship at Swathmore, they sent me word that Bruce would be barred from the course during the play. Of course I knew that none but the caddies or players in your own match are allowed to help you find your ball, but I had always gotten by on this rule with Bruce by claiming that the rule referred to persons and had no bearing on dogs. I'd always figured that if it ever came to a real showdown I'd claim the right to take Bruce along as a fore caddie. But here, now, came notice of a special ruling of the committee, made particularly and directly just to bar Bruce.

"This was mighty bad news for me, for I was playing that year the best golf I've ever played, and I thought I had a good chance for the championship. But it had become such a habit with me to have Bruce along, and I had gotten to depend on him so, that I felt I'd be lost

Facing page: *American cockers—one wide awake, the other sound asleep.* Photograph © Sharon Eide/ Elizabeth Flynn

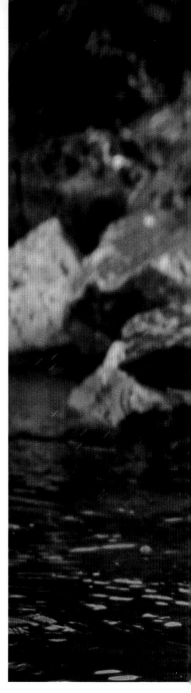

without him.

"For a week or more I debated what to do—then I hit upon a plan. I wrote to the committee and said that I expected to play in the tournament and that I would be unaccompanied except by my caddie.

"Of course they wrote me that this was satisfactory and they were glad I felt right about it," and, as he told this, Sandy could not hide a quiet smile. His eyes showed merriment as he recalled the event. But I said not a word to interrupt the story.

"I didn't get to Swathmore until the opening day of the tournament, as I didn't want the committee to have time to make any more moves against me. But of course, when I did arrive and they saw Bruce, there was a howl went up.

"'Didn't you understand that you weren't to bring that dog?' they asked.

"'No, I didn't understand that,' I told them.

"'We thought we wrote you,' they said.

"'You wrote me that Bruce couldn't go along with me during play, as he's been doing—that you'd ruled he'd have to be considered same as anyone else on the outside and not allowed to go along and help my caddie find my balls.'

"'Well, isn't that plain enough?' they wanted to know.

"'Yes,' I told them, 'but *he's to be my caddie*—the only one I'll have—and you wrote me I'd be entitled to one caddie same as anyone else. Well, he's my caddie, that's all.'

"You see, Mr. Welty, I'd kinda outplayed 'em in a way they hadn't looked for. Any player is allowed to have a caddie, and there's nothing in the rules that says whether he must be man, boy, or beast. I realized that they could keep me from having Bruce go along as he'd been doing when I had a caddie too; but if I didn't take any other caddie along—that was different. I had them up a tree, and they knew it. They tried to figure up some way to rule Bruce out, but after a bit they gave it up."

"I guess you were right about that point, too, Sandy," I said, "I can see how they could rule Bruce from the course during play, as a dog—but as your one and only caddie, you had them, didn't you?"

"Sure," answered Sandy, "and here's the point: Bruce was worth any ten caddies at finding the ball, and that might mean more to me in a match than having some kid carry my clubs. Just one lost ball might

lose a match—that's how I figured. And that's the way it would have turned out. I'll tell you about the match for the championship and the part Bruce played in it, then I'll have to go back to the shop and get ready to give another lesson. Old Bruce helped me win a lot of matches in his day, but I'll only have time to tell you about the one—for to-day, at least."

"Go ahead, Sandy, and by then I'll have to be getting back to the office, too. Press the button there and we'll have the boy bring us another pot of coffee while you're telling the rest."

"The night before the finals, at the Swathmore Club," continued Sandy, "there was considerable speculation on the match to be played next day. Much interest was added from the fact that a dog, for the first time in the history of golf, was to be the official caddie in a champion-

*By the side of a lake, an English springer spaniel is ready to retrieve.*
Photograph © Judith E. Strom

ship. You see, Mr. Welty, I had played through to the finals. There was more interest than is common even in championships—due, you understand, largely to Bruce—and the betting ran high.

"I guess you must realize that I loved Bruce just like he was human—and he did me, too. He seemed to feel, that night, the importance of what was coming off for us both next day, and he hardly wanted to eat when I brought him his supper, and he just kept right at my heels and looking up at me much as to say it would be all right and not to worry. He did a lot to help me keep my nerve. I tell you, Mr. Welty, there didn't any of you 'round here ever realize what a dog Bruce was. If you could only have seen him when he was young!

"I was going to go to bed early, so as to be fit next day to play and carry the clubs for thirty-six holes, but I left Bruce in my room and went out to get a cigar. This happened just when there was considerable money being placed on the game. One young fellow asked sarcastically what I'd take for my dog.

"'He ain't for sale,' I told him, 'but he's worth more than you'd pay for him.'

"Of course he didn't like that very much, the way I said it, and he came back at me pretty strong. One thing led to another, and before long we were both talking pretty stiff language. It got personal, and he said I didn't have a chance to win anyhow, dog or no dog.

"'For how much?' I asked him.

"'Oh, say fifty dollars,' he said.

"I was kinda mad anyhow, so I answered, 'Better make it a hundred.'

"And that's where I got in hot water. The young shrimp had more money than brains.

"'So you really want to bet, I see,' he said. 'Then let's make it a thousand.'

"Now, that was more money than I could afford to bet, as you may well imagine, Mr. Welty. In fact, it was all the money I had in the world. But I was mad all through—so mad that I lost my head, and I said to him, 'All right, we'll make it an even thousand.'

"It took me a long time to get to sleep that night. What if I should lose—and I knew that, on dope, I stood more chance to lose than to win. Anderson was an older player than I, with more match experience; and besides that, he was already the Champion. What if I lost my thousand dollars! I had enough at stake to play for, without the money end of it that I had gotten myself into. I just couldn't sleep, even though I knew that I ought to, to be in fit shape the next day. I tossed and tossed. Then I called Bruce from his pillow in the corner, right into bed with me. He curled up close, and I put my arm around him. Something in his presence gave me comfort and assurance—and rest. By being near me he seemed to make me feel it would be all right—and I finally fell asleep.

"When I awoke the next morning, Bruce had not moved. He

Facing page: *The American water spaniel was likely a cross between the Irish water spaniel and a smaller spaniel and a curly-coated retriever. Whatever the gene pool, the breed is spectacular.* Photograph © Kent and Donna Dannen

*A Clumber spaniel twosome with only one thing on their minds.* Photograph © Isabelle Francais

licked my hand when I petted him and he saw that I was awake. As soon as I was ready to get up, I went straight to the showers—and let the water come cold. Then I felt almost as fit as if I'd had a better night's sleep.

"After breakfast I sat down and tried to read, to get my mind off the game. But it was a hard job. I determined that I *must* conquer my shaky nerves. What if I lost? Then I tried to console myself with the thought that that was the worst I could do—and what of it! Mine wasn't the only money in the world. Of course it would be hard for a while, but what of that?

"This was the way I made myself figure it out, and it helped me a lot. By the time we were ready to tee up for the morning round, I was in the right mood to play good golf. The actual fact of losing couldn't possibly upset me more than I had been the night before, just in anticipation—so I had already gone through the worst, which nothing more could equal. And the assurance coming with that thought was cool and refreshing.

"I couldn't seem to get to hitting them the first nine, but even at that was only two down. This gave me confidence, and coming in, I evened up the match. In fact, I was one up going to the eighteenth hole, but lost that.

"It was just the kind of hole I like, however, and I made a vow to myself that I wouldn't lose that last hole in the afternoon. It was about four hundred and fifty yards, straight away across a ravine with a necessary carry on the drive of more than a hundred and sixty yards, if you would even hope to reach the fairway for a good lie. To the right there was trouble, but to the left it was infinitely worse—in fact, a hooked ball would be next to impossible to play. The green was in an open space, surrounded by trees on the right, left and behind. The ground sloped off to the left into a gully. The hope of success lay in a straight ball on your second shot with your brassie or iron. I lost the hole by slicing just enough to get in among the trees to the right, and it cost me a stroke coming out. Anderson had reached the edge of the green with his second and played an easy four to beat my five.

"'That's one hole I won't lose this afternoon,' I promised myself, for, as I've said, it was really the kind of hole I like to play.'"

"Well, did you lose it in the afternoon?" I ventured to ask.

"I'm going to tell you about it," he answered. "The fact that I had broken even at the turn gave me confidence, and by the time we had finished lunch all my nervousness had left. I seemed to forget about the bet, in my interest in the match. Something made me think it was going to be my day. I felt that I could win, and you know how much that means in golf.

"Well, in the afternoon we were followed by the largest gallery I've ever played to. And it was some match, Mr. Welty. Confident as I was, Anderson must have been equally so, for it was nip and tuck all the way. We were all even at the twenty-seventh, and then halved the next six holes in succession.

"I didn't lose my nerve until the thirty-fourth, which I lost, making me one down and two to play. Then, had Anderson played carefully and safe, it would have been all over for me. But he got over-confident and tried to beat me on the thirty-fifth with a win, instead of being satisfied with a halve. Anyhow, he pressed his tee shot—and dubbed it into a bad lie.

"Had he gotten a good drive, Mr. Welty, I know he'd have had my nerve. But when he dubbed his drive, for the first time in the match, it just put me right back on my feet—and I won that hole easily, going all even to the thirty-sixth. And that's the hole I was telling you about.

"We both got good drives, but I had about fifteen yards the advantage. Anderson was short on his second, and I tried to reach the green with my spoon. I not only overplayed, but pulled it—the worst thing I could have done on that hole. The last we saw of the ball was when it hit a tree—and none of us could tell which way it glanced. It looked like a lost hole—and match—for me all right, for even if Bruce could

Overleaf: *A true spaniel is the Clumber, though a touch of Basset hound is obviously in their bloodlines.* Photograph © Isabelle Francais

find it, there was that impossible gully just where the ball struck the tree. Anderson, of course, laid his third well up to the hole, but not close enough to be dead for a sure four. But where was I in two! That was the big question.

"Bruce worked in the gully for that ball as he never had done before. He seemed to realize how much was at stake, and he fairly swept the ground clean. But we couldn't find the ball! It was almost hopeless in such a place to expect to find it—more so to play it afterwards. Almost four minutes were gone, and I decided that the ball was not in the gully. But where, then? None of us had seen the direction it had taken off the tree. I called Bruce in and gave him the command: 'Range, boy—range.' That meant that he was to work in a circle and cover as much ground as possible. And he fairly flew, Mr. Welty. You'd have given a hundred dollars just to have seen him.

"'The five minutes is—'

"'Wait!' I called, before the sentence could be completed. 'My caddie has the ball.'

"Bruce had just whined—and he was standing on point. We went to him—and there was my ball sure enough, just on the edge of the rough to the right, and not a bad lie at that, and a clear shot for the hole. You see, the ball had glanced off the tree to the right, instead of to the left into the gully, as we had naturally supposed. But if it hadn't been for Bruce it'd have been a lost ball for good, for it would never have occurred to us to look where he found it, and it'd have cost me both the match and my bet."

"You won then, eh?" I asked, as the boy handed me our lunch ticket to sign.

"Oh, yes—it was easy to lay my third shot dead for a four; and Anderson missed his putt."

I looked at Sandy and could see in his eyes the faintest suggestion of a moisture that he could not hide, as his mind went back to that day, and to the wonderful performance of his devoted dog.

"I grabbed Bruce up in my arms, Mr. Welty, and hugged him right there—before everyone. It was he—not I—who had saved the match, and *won for me a thousand dollars!* Do you wonder, now, why I feel as I always have about Bruce?"

"No—I should say not, Sandy," and I was conscious of a strong pull on my own heartstrings, as I saw how deeply the Scotchman felt.

And later, when I told this story to the crowd on Saturday, as nearly as possible as Sandy had told it to me, they all agreed—and Jim himself freely admitted—that he owed me a box of balls.

*A Clumber spaniel relaxing after a hard day's work.* Photograph © Tara Darling

# *About the Editor*

Todd R. Berger is the editor of the anthologies *Love of Labs, Love of Goldens, Love of Dogs, Love of German Shepherds,* and three others on outdoors subjects. He is the acquisitions editor for Voyageur Press and a Minnesota-based freelance writer. *Photograph © Tim Berger*